Tributes
Tributes
Tributes
Tributes
Tributes
Tributes
Tributes
Tributes
Tributes
Tributes
Tributes
Tributes
Tributes
Tributes
Tributes
Tributes
Tributes

Tributes

Remembering Some of
the World's Greatest Wrestlers

Dave Meltzer

WrestLiNgObserver

WINDING
STAIR
PRESS

National Library of Canada Cataloguing in Publication Data

Meltzer, Dave
        The Wrestling observer's Tributes: remembering some of the world's greatest wrestlers

Previously published under title: Tributes.
ISBN 1-55366-085-4

        1. Wrestlers – Obituaries. I. Tributes.

GV1196.AIM44 2001   796.812'092'2   C2001-902403-7

Winding Stair Press
An imprint of Stewart House Publishing Inc.
Etobicoke, Ontario
www.stewarthousepub.com
Executive Vice President and Publisher: Ken Proctor
Director of Publishing and Product Acquisition: Joe March

1   2   3   4   5   05   04   03   02   01

We would like to thank Sully's Gym in Toronto for access to their wrestling and boxing ring for the front cover photo.
Book design by Counterpunch / Peter Ross

This book is available at special discounts for bulk purchases by groups or organizations for sales promotions, premiums, fundraising and educational purposes. For details, contact: Peter March, Stewart House Publishing Inc., Special Sales Department, 195 Allstate Parkway, Markham, Ontario. Tel: (866) 474-3478.

Printed and bound in Canada

INTERIOR PHOTOGRAPHS: ©Bill Janosik, ©Dr. Michael Lano, ©Bob Leonard, and ©George Napolitano.

Every effort has been made to contact copyright holders. In the event of omission or error the publisher should be notified.

Photo credits in page order:

x: Dr. Michael Lano. 1: Dr. Michael Lano. 2: Bob Leonard. 3: Bob Leonard. 4: Dr. Michael Lano. 5: Dr. Michael Lano. 6: Dr. Michael Lano. 7: George Napolitano. 8: Bob Leonard. 9: Bob Leonard. 11: Bob Leonard. 12: George Napolitano. 13: Dr. Michael Lano. 14: Dr. Michael Lano. 16: George Napolitano. 18: Bob Leonard. 19: Bob Leonard. 20: Dr. Michael Lano. 21: Dr. Michael Lano. 22: Bob Leonard. 23: Bob Leonard. 24: Dr. Michael Lano. 25: (top and bottom) George Napolitano. 26: Dr. Michael Lano. 27: George Napolitano. 28: Dr. Michael Lano. 30: Dr. Michael Lano. 31: George Napolitano. 32: George Napolitano. 33: George Napolitano. 34: George Napolitano. 36: George Napolitano. 38: George Napolitano. 39: George Napolitano. 40: (top and bottom) Bob Leonard. 41: Bob Leonard. 42: George Napolitano. 43: George Napolitano. 44: Bob Leonard. 45: Bob Leonard. 46: George Napolitano. 47: George Napolitano. 48: George Napolitano. 49: George Napolitano. 50: George Napolitano. 51: Bob Leonard. 52: Dr. Michael Lano. 54: George Napolitano. 55: George Napolitano. 56: Dr. Michael Lano. 58: Dr. Michael Lano. 59: George Napolitano. 60: George Napolitano. 62: Bob Leonard. 65: George Napolitano. 66: Dr. Michael Lano. 67: Dr. Michael Lano. 69: Dr. Michael Lano. 70: George Napolitano. 72: George Napolitano. 74: George Napolitano. 75: Dr. Michael Lano. 76: George Napolitano. 77: George Napolitano. 78: George Napolitano. 79: Dr. Michael Lano. 80: George Napolitano. 82: Dr. Michael Lano. 83: George Napolitano. 84: Dr. Michael Lano. 85: George Napolitano. 86: George Napolitano. 87: George Napolitano. 88: Dr. Michael Lano. 89: Dr. Michael Lano. 90: Dr. Michael Lano. 91: Dr. Michael Lano. 92: Dr. Michael Lano. 94: Dr. Michael Lano. 95: Dr. Michael Lano. 96: Bob Leonard. 97: Bob Leonard. 98: Bob Leonard. 99: Bob Leonard. 100: Bob Leonard. 102: Bob Leonard. 103: Dr. Michael Lano. 104: Bob Leonard. 106: Dr. Michael Lano. 109: Dr. Michael Lano. 110: Dr. Michael Lano. 111: Dr. Michael Lano. 112: Dr. Michael Lano. 114: Bob Leonard. 116: Bob Leonard. 118: Dr. Michael Lano. 119: Bob Leonard. 120: George Napolitano. 122: Dr. Michael Lano. 124: George Napolitano. 125: George Napolitano. 126: George Napolitano. 128: Dr. Michael Lano. 130: (top and bottom) Dr. Michael Lano. 131: Bob Leonard. 132: Bob Leonard. 133: Dr. Michael Lano. 134: Dr. Michael Lano. 135: Dr. Michael Lano. 136: Dr. Michael Lano. 137: Dr. Michael Lano. 138: Dr. Michael Lano. 139: Dr. Michael Lano. 140: Dr. Michael Lano. 141: Funeral card (courtesy Dr. Michael Lano). 142: Dr. Michael Lano. 144: Dr. Michael Lano. 145: Dr. Michael Lano. 146: Dr. Michael Lano. 147: Dr. Michael Lano. 148: Dr. Michael Lano. 150: George Napolitano. 151: Dr. Michael Lano. 152: Dr. Michael Lano. 153: Dr. Michael Lano. 154: George Napolitano. 155: Dr. Michael Lano. 156: Dr. Michael Lano. 157: Dr. Michael Lano. 158: Bill Janosik. 160: Bill Janosik. 164: Bill Janosik. 165: Bill Janosik. 166. Bill Janosik. 167. George Napolitano. 168. George Napolitano. 174: Dr. Michael Lano. 176: Dr. Michael Lano. 177: Dr. Michael Lano.

DEDICATION

I would like to dedicate this book to all of the readers of the *Wrestling Observer Newsletter*, who have given me so much inspiration to persevere and cover pro wrestling for what it really is for the past two decades; to my parents, Marilyn and Herb Meltzer; and to my fiancée, Mary Anne Mirabal, for putting up with all the hours of pro wrestling from all corners of the world constantly on television.

ACKNOWLEDGEMENTS

There are so many people to thank for this book being possible, from Larry Weaver and Ted Hopgood, who came up with the original idea, to Jeff Marek, Sam Galet and everyone at Thin Data, Live Audio Wrestling and Stewart House Publishing for the finished product.

I'd like to thank so many people who have helped me along the way. There are many who need to be singled out, including Larry Matysik, Bill Watts and Bruiser Brody, who were the first people in the wrestling industry to accept coverage of wrestling for what it really was and who taught me to see past the con games. The late Paul Boesch, who pushed the idea of learning about the history of wrestling, something that really didn't exist except in the faded memories of the participants at the time. I'd like to thank Gary Will and all the people who have helped him over the years in attempting to formulate some sort of a history of a business that really never existed.

I'd like to thank Kim Wood, for being such an inspiration in writing; Bryan Alvarez of Figure Four Weekly for making me laugh so much; Al Gatullo, for partnering for 22 months in doing the best radio wrestling show around; Frank Deford, who gave me my first mainstream break at a time when real sports people were supposed to look down their noses at pro wrestling; Alex Marvez, who learned from pro wrestling to become one of the best football writers in the country; and Bruce Mitchell, for his input as we constantly try to figure out where this strange industry is headed next.

There are many others in wrestling who, unfortunately, still to this day, would get in political hot water for being mentioned, but hopefully they know who they are. I'd also like to thank Mick Foley, for not only writing two best-sellers, but writing two lengthy books on wrestling, and mostly, for disproving the stigma we've all had to live with – that wrestling fans can't read.

Contents

FOREWORD

Professional wrestling is not as strange a creature as many would think – like any other sport, it is totally contingent on its past for its future. Without its own history fully digested, the industry is doomed to repeat the same mistakes. And the sad truth is, it does repeat those mistakes, time and time again. Nowhere is this more obvious than in how the wrestling industry handles the passing of its performers.

We all know the people in this book because we see them on TV. Fans generally think of them, not as real human beings, but as heroes and "special" people who don't live with the same realities we do. This is, of course, a total fiction, but one that promoters would rather the fans believe.

For those of us who follow wrestling closely, each wrestler's passing, however sad and at times tragically predictable, always brings with it the opportunity for change, even in an unforgiving and uncaring industry.

I wish I could write about how the industry has changed with every wrestler's passing, but I can't do that. The reality of how death is handled by the various promotions is a ten-bell salute and maybe a mention on TV. Then it's on with the show. If it does anything, wrestling bows its head momentarily to acknowledge the passing then quickly goes about the business of hyping the next card. There are no memorial tournaments or titles named after wrestlers who have gone before, which is quite unlike traditional sports where trophies, teams and arenas are named after the people who created and sustained their respective sports. This is the tie that binds those sports to their pasts. Wrestling, however, seems to go out of its way to shatter that bond.

The brief exception to this rule was the case of Owen Hart, which was such a huge mainstream media spectacle that the WWF had to devote more than just a few minutes of its precious TV time to his passing. Still, nothing was explained about how or why he died.

In my four and a half years of hosting a wrestling radio show in Toronto, Canada, I've learned that no matter how much the wrestling promotions try to ignore their own history, the questions are still there and go unanswered. What happened? How did it happen? The questions never stop, and probably never will. There is no place where wrestling fans can learn about the reality of wrestling, the lives it shatters and leaves behind in its quest for a bigger gate, higher ticket price, elevated pay-per-view buy rate or TV ratings.

Although few will talk about it publicly for fear of punishment from their promoters, just about every wrestler I talk to is disgusted with the way their industry handles death.

Tributes is not about a morbid fascination with the deaths of pro wrestlers, as some have claimed, rather it is a book that lends some much-needed dignity to wrestlers whose own industry generally affords them very little, if any, respect.

In the following pages, you will read about the lives and deaths of some of the most interesting and often controversial performers in the history of the wrestling business, including:

Owen Hart, not as the Blue Blazer but as the father and concerned citizen who was torn between providing for his family and mortgaging his soul to a company whose product he profoundly disagreed with.

André Rousimoff, who was lovingly called the Giant by fans who flocked to see him all over the world, yet who secretly lived a life of alcohol abuse and intense physical pain.

Brian Pillman, whose death provoked shame in those around him who sat back, watched and did nothing. Pillman's death still haunts many wrestlers you see on TV each and every week.

Bruiser Brody, whom many consider the best "big man" wrestler of all time and who was slaughtered in Puerto Rico by a fellow wrestler who was never brought to justice. Worse still is how his murderer became a feared villain and was marketed to the wrestling audience as "the man who killed Brody."

Eddie Gilbert, who became so consumed by the phoniness of the industry it made him inherently untrusting of everyone around him, and whose intense paranoia fueled his drug addiction.

Shohei "Giant" Baba, not only considered a Japanese cultural icon but also a man many believed to be the rarest creature in the wrestling industry – an honest promoter.

Gordon Solie, a sane voice in a seemingly insane world, generally acknowledged as the premiere voice of professional wrestling and who defined what it meant to call a wrestling match.

Kerry Von Erich, from the famous Von Erich family, who was born into fame and status, which simultaneously created and destroyed him.

Pro wrestling exaggerates its characters to make them seem larger than life in a never-ending quest to make fans suspend disbelief and buy the product. In *Tributes*, you'll read about people, human beings you may have once thought of only as performers, acts and characters in a circus that never seems to end. These are the real stories of their lives. There is no exaggeration or hyperbole in these pages. There doesn't have to be. In a world where "truth" is a bad word and performers are encouraged to ignore and downplay the reality of what's going on around them, the truth is the most fascinating and revealing part of these people's lives. There is no wrestling storyline that can compare to what you're about to read.

Jeff Marek, September 2001

It's almost ironic. From Owen Hart's first few matches as a full-time pro wrestler in the spring of 1986, it seemed apparent he would achieve great fame and become a pivotal figure in the history of this industry. And he did, in a way nobody could ever have guessed.

Sunday, May 23, 1999, 7:41 PM Central Time. In one of the most famous moments of modern wrestling history, Jim Ross was setting to pitch a pre-taped interview with Owen Hart under the mask as the Blue Blazer. Just before the tape ran he said, "We've got a big problem out here." The tape of Owen Hart's last interview ran anyway.

Unbeknownst to the audience watching on pay-per-view, Jerry Lawler ran into the ring immediately. The big problem was that Owen Hart, in his Blue Blazer costume, was coming down from a scaffold near the ceiling of Kemper Arena in Kansas City to do a spectacular ring entrance – a spoof on Sting. And somehow he slipped out of his harness, falling headfirst to land on a turnbuckle and flip into the ring. Those at ringside watching said it was clear he had a broken neck. Many in the audience thought it was a crash test dummy, and part of the show. The cameras were on the crowd, standing, in stunned silence. They wouldn't shoot anywhere near the ring.

Ross said that something went terribly wrong. In a line that may become the single most famous uttered at a pro wrestling event in modern history, Ross also said, "This is not part of the entertainment portion of the show. This is as real as real can get."

As emergency medical technicians feverishly tried heart massage, those at ringside could hear the panic because Hart had no pulse. He was changing color rapidly. First he went white, then grey, then purple and finally blue. They tried mouth-to-mouth. They tried to put on an oxygen mask. As they showed the crowd, never once getting a shot of the EMTs working on Hart, fans at ringside in the building could see Ross teary eyed. Some still thought this was all part of the show. Lawler, with his face white as a ghost, came back to the broadcast location. As people who know Jerry Lawler would attest, even when he's out of character, he's always "on". Not this time, as he somberly said, "It doesn't look good at all." Hart was wheeled backstage on a stretcher. Not another word was said again about it on television for an hour. Nothing was ever said to the live audience at Kemper Arena the rest of the night.

The show must go on. Yeah, right. This was an issue hotly debated by wrestling fans who vehemently argued

OWEN POSED BACKSTAGE FOR HIS U.S. DEBUT, *RIGHT:* OWEN WINS THE INTERNATIONAL CHAMPIONSHIP IN 1995 – HOLDS THE TITLE FOR ONLY A FEW MINUTES UNTIL THE DECISION IS REVERSED

A YOUTHFUL OWEN HART WITH THE NORTH AMERICAN HEAVYWEIGHT CHAMPIONSHIP BELT (IN HIS RIGHT HAND) AND THE BRITISH COMMONWEALTH MID-HEAVYWEIGHT CHAMPIONSHIP BELT. HE HELD THE TWO TITLES SIMULTANEOUSLY. (JAN 1987), *FACING PAGE:* BATTERED AND BLOODY, OWEN LEAVES THE RING WITH THE NORTH AMERICAN HEAVYWEIGHT CHAMPIONSHIP AFTER A CAGE MATCH (1988)

▶ **The wwf was brutalized in the media** over the next few days by people shocked at what was perceived as their callous disregard for human life. There are arguments that can be made in both directions. But in examining them, the case for continuing the show after Owen Hart's death is weak. This was a snap decision under an incredible amount of stress, and there are precedents on both sides. The 1972 Olympics weren't cancelled when the Israeli athletes were massacred. And there have been auto races that have continued after a driver has been killed. Most other sports, including pro and college football, baseball and basketball have set precedents that games don't continue if a participant dies on the field. But even those arguments don't hold because, by its own admission and its attempt to categorize and position itself as an entertainment spectacle, pro wrestling is not a sporting event. There was already a precedent a few years back at the infamous wwf Beware of Dog ppv show. Due to weather conditions and a power failure, several of the matches didn't take place. They finished the missing part of the show two days later.

both sides. In the real world, just the idea that fans would think that there was a decision to be made emphasized their view of just how sick a profession this must be. ▶

Just before all this was going on in front of the fans at Kemper Arena, Vince McMahon was setting up a scene where he'd be on a stretcher and "taken to the hospital" in an ambulance. While Pat Patterson and Gerald Brisco did their comedy routine, McMahon was put in the ambulance and driven away. As it was pulling out and the scene was cut, Bruce Prichard screamed to them that something had happened and that the ambulance needed to come back. Because Hart had just died, doing a mock angle where McMahon would be taken out in an ambulance would be in the worst possible taste. But

then it was also in the script, and apparently nothing – certainly not good taste and apparently not even death – was going to make them overlook key points in the show.

Would anyone have complained if they simply announced the show was over due to the tragedy, and would be rescheduled for Tuesday? They certainly didn't cancel the scheduled show on Tuesday in Moline. Why was the death not announced to the live crowd in the building? And why did the announcers distinctly, except for a brief mention of Hart's death one hour after it happened, never mention his name, his condition, or say anything else about him to a stunned television audience for the rest of the show?

Owen Hart was born May 7, 1965. Nearly every wrestling fan knows the place. Most even know the house. He was the youngest of a family of eight boys and four girls. All eight boys became wrestlers. All four girls married them. It's definitely not what their mother had in mind.

ABOVE AND FACING PAGE: OWEN HART IN HIS U.S. DEBUT VS. NEW JAPAN'S
TAKAYUKI IZUKA IN PHILADELPHIA

He was always around wrestling. It was his father's
life. All his brothers did it. Older wrestlers who were superstars of the early '70s tell stories about five-year-old Owen
running barefoot in the snow. Or eight-year-old Owen
helping older brother Bruce write the wrestling programs.
Or 14-year-old Owen, accompanying big brothers Bruce
and Keith to a show in Honolulu where they played heel
against a huge, untalented Samoan tag team in a building
with inadequate security and rabid Samoan fans. The
brothers, used to playing face at home, were a little too
effective playing heel and a riot broke out. A few attacked
Bruce and Keith, who were doing a decent job holding
them off. A large adult Samoan fan threw a chair at Keith.
Owen, totally undersized, jumped right in the fray and
wound up with a black eye.

As a child, he shared a room with three of his brothers: Ross, who was five years older, Bret, who was eight
years older, and Dean, who was ten years older. But the
biggest influence on him was Bruce, 15 years his senior,
who taught him the world of practical jokes that among
wrestlers made him famous. All his brothers tried
wrestling with varying degrees of success. Keith and
Bruce went to college first and got their teaching credentials, but wound up working in their father's wrestling
business. Bret, who at first never wanted to be a wrestler,
one day wound up in the ring, turned out to be pretty
good and never stopped. Ross, who loved being on the
road with the boys but didn't have the athletic ability of his
more famous brothers, wound up working backstage and
occasionally wrestling. Owen, growing up, was the best
athlete of all the boys, and thus became Stu's favorite.

He would goof around the ring as a teenager, and he
picked everything up quickly. He never did gymnastics,
but one day he decided to do a backflip off the turnbuck-
les to set up a hip-toss spot. He tried it with a spotter
once, hit the move perfectly, and never needed a spotter

again. It was like that with every move. He grew up seeing legends like the Funk Brothers and Harley Race come through Stampede Wrestling as touring NWA world champions, all the great British wrestlers from Billy Robinson to the Dynamite Kid, and young Japanese stars as well. He learned to mix all the various styles and even threw in some Lucha Libre at a time when nobody in wrestling learned any style other than what was done in their own local territory. As early as the age of 16, Owen wrestled under a mask in small towns in the middle of nowhere, since it had to be kept secret to maintain his amateur wrestling eligibility. He'd fill in on shows and his brothers remember him being a natural. He played varsity baseball, football and wrestled at Ernest Manning High School, becoming city and Alberta provincial high school champion in 1983 at 165 pounds. By this point he was also watching a lot of Japanese wrestling videotapes, since Bret was a major junior heavyweight star there, and Dynamite Kid, the greatest worker in the promotion and possibly the world at the time, was becoming legendary in the Orient. Hart studied the matches from the original Tiger Mask, the most innovative high flier of his era, and later, The Cobra. At a

school dance in late 1982, he met Martha Patterson, whom he fell hard for and eventually married.

After graduating high school in 1983, he accompanied brother Ross on a wrestling tour of Europe. Ross was going there as a wrestler. Owen was going there because he had a chance to spend the summer after graduation in Europe. Just before leaving, there was an injury in the crew and Owen, under a mask to protect both kayfabe and his amateur eligibility, formed a tag team with Dynamite Kid against Ross and a wrestler named Gary Eichenhauser. Owen totally outshined his brother and they were quickly made a tag team. By the time they went to England for Joint Promotions, Owen was using his real name, since wrestling news from England was hardly in danger of making its way to the collegiate authorities in Canada. He was an immediate star after wrestling a classic 40 minute television match against Marty Jones and feuding with a veteran star named David "Fit" Finlay.

"Nobody pushed him into it," remembered Ross. "We all knew from the start he was a natural talent. He was never that anxious to make it a career. He just wanted to do it to see how it was. I never had the talent of

a skilled wrestler like Owen and Bret, but he always encouraged me and made me feel good. But I was so happy to see him follow Bruce, Bret and Keith."

Owen Hart, now a teenage pro sensation in England, returned home for his freshman year at the University of Calgary. He was studying for his teaching credentials, following in the footsteps of brothers Bruce and Keith, both of whom at the time were wrestling for Stampede. He was a very good college wrestler, and in fact, was never once pinned in three years of collegiate varsity competition, although he lost a few matches, mostly via close decisions.

At around this same time, Vince McMahon was attempting to become the only wrestling promoter in North America, if not the world. Some territories he bulldozed. A few he avoided until later. He tried to buy a few, and was rebuffed. The only one who took him up on his offer was Stu Hart. He was 68 years old and, unlike many of his compadres who wound up out of business, knew he didn't have the money or the strength to fight McMahon. The two agreed to a deal where McMahon would pay Hart $100,000 per year for ten years, plus hire Stu as his local promoter for shows in Calgary and Edmonton, with Stu getting 10% of the gate in each city. As part of the deal, Stu talked Vince into giving a job to his three biggest stars, his son Bret, his future son-in-law Davey Boy Smith, and Dynamite Kid. All three were already stars in Japan with Dynamite on the verge of being a legend. Kid and Smith lasted only a few weeks, with no push, in the WWF (World Wrestling Foundation) before quitting to take a deal with All Japan. (They ended up back several months later, this time with a push, and became forever more known as the British Bulldogs.) Bret stayed, and in the beginning, also got no push. According to Bruce Hart, it didn't take long for McMahon to renege on the annual payments. One year later Stampede Wrestling was re-opened.

As a sophomore, Owen went to the CIAU (Canadian collegiate amateurs) nationals and placed third at 177 pounds. When he considered going into pro wrestling, his father strongly discouraged it. Stu loved pro wrestling, but as a great amateur himself and a two-time national champion in the late '30s, he was a total aficionado for what was real and wanted one of his sons to wrestle in the Olympics. Everyone knows the stories about him stretching big weightlifters and football play-

 One of the most well-rounded wrestlers ever, Owen Hart, *facing page:* Owen vs. Scott (Razor Ramon) Hall in a WWF match

ers downstairs in the famed dungeon. Stu wanted his sons to be tough guys and great amateurs, but they simply weren't, at least on that level. He wanted Bret, also a provincial champion, to continue on as an amateur and fulfill Stu's dream of going to the Olympics, but Bret gave up amateur wrestling after high school. Owen would be the last son. During his junior year, he placed second in the CIAU nationals at 177 pounds, but after that season, the University of Calgary shut down its wrestling program and Owen was off scholarship. A few weeks later, Owen Hart, without a mask, under his own name, and in his home town of Calgary, made his pro debut, and was an instant success.

Owen and Bruce were supposed to become the headline tag team for Stampede. As it turned out, Bruce blew out his knee and needed major surgery and was out for ten months. A brother-in-law, Ben Bassarab, filled in and formed a team with Owen and they quickly became the international tag team champions, having a still legendary feud against the masked Viet Cong Express – Hiroshi Hase who was already a great worker in his first pro match,

IT LOOKS LIKE A BACKDROP, BUT OWEN PINIONS THE ARMS OF VIET CONG
EXPRESS NO. 1 AND THEN DROPS ON TOP OF HIM FOR A PINFALL (1987)
FACING PAGE: OWEN IN FULL FLIGHT, DIVING ONTO VIET CONG EXPRESS
NO. 1 (1987)

and Fumihiro Niikura, who was actually even better then Hase at the time. The teams were having the best matches in North America, and Hart was, within a few weeks of his debut, already the biggest star in the company.

"He was sensational from day one," recalled Bruce. "He had all the moves, and the timing and psychology." The two teams fought many lengthy matches over the tag team titles, which later led to Hart vs. Hase under a mask as a feud which was reprised in New Japan the next year. When Hase returned to Japan as the top junior heavyweight in the promotion, he brought in Hart as his favorite opponent for several tours, including a brief period when Hart held the IWGP junior heavyweight title, the first foreigner ever to do so. Hart had only been a pro for a few months but his reputation as one of the most spectacular wrestlers in the business began spreading. The WWF offered him a deal after he was brought in

for a weekend tour in California and stunned everyone (under the name Owen James). The money was tempting, but he turned it down, wanting to spend the weekends with Martha.

Eventually, upon prodding from Bret, Davey, Dynamite and Jim Neidhart, Owen changed his mind and went to the WWF as a masked high flier, patterned after Tiger Mask.

Vince called him The American Eagle, The Blue Angel, The Blue Demon, The Blue Lazer and finally settled on the Blue Blazer. On the inside, he was known as the Blue Sports Coat. Although he went over very strong initially with his spectacular work, particularly with young children, the company didn't have eyes for a guy who was 5'9" and 210 pounds. He got no push and eventually fans caught on that he wasn't a star. He started losing heat, and then started jobbing. Many times he came close to quitting, because he felt his development as a wrestler was going backwards and because he didn't like how he was being used. His father would always tell him to stick it out. At the time he was rooming on the road with Ultimate Warrior. The two came in at about the same time and Jim Hellwig, with a monster push and limited ability, got over amazingly strong in the era of steroids. Hart finally decided to quit. At the time Hellwig was also looking to quit and work full-time in Japan, as Hart was talking about doing. Hart figured he'd save money there since the promotion pays for hotels and travel in Japan, and he'd have more time off the road. He'd actually come out of the year with the same money for less days away from home and he'd have more good matches in the process. But Hart convinced Hellwig that Japan isn't for everyone and he'd be better off staying put. ▶

In late 1991, Owen returned to the WWF just as Bret was becoming a major star. Wearing suspenders and baggy clown pants he formed a tag team with Koko B. Ware called "High Energy." Going back to the WWF was not his first choice. He had gotten married to Martha on July 1, 1989 and bought his first home. He tried to get into the Calgary Fire Department, with the idea that it would be a steady job since Stampede Wrestling was closing down, and he'd continue to do Japanese tours. But couldn't get on, so with mixed emotions, he went back to the WWF.

Owen was stuck in openers, except for a period when

they put him with Jim Neidhart as the New Hart Foundation with a medium push. Bret had long since outgrown tag team wrestling and was being groomed for a top singles spot with the company. Bret, who didn't want to do the family feud idea again because he wasn't happy doing it so publicly with Davey Boy Johnson a few years earlier, finally relented. They did the angle starting at a Survivor Series match. Keith and Bruce were brought in, and Stu was put at ringside, to team with Owen and Bret against Shawn Michaels and three masked wrestlers (Jeff Gaylord, Barry Horowitz and Greg Valentine). Owen lost the only fall for his team and ended up turning on the entire family. For months, reminiscent of Undertaker vs. Kane but more realistic, they teased a break-up with Bret refusing to wrestle him. They then teased being put back together, to set up their first meeting with Bret putting Owen over at Wrestlemania x on March 20, 1994 at Madison Square Garden. It was the opening match of the show and was one of his two or three best matches with the company. It was actually among the greatest bouts in company history – a show which later ended with Bret winning the wwf title from Yokozuna.

Owen beating Bret just hours before Bret won the title left Owen vs. Bret as the big summer feud in the wwf. This was a period when the wwf business was in the toilet, but the Bret vs. Owen run after Wrestlemania for the title did the biggest house business since the bottom fell out in 1992.

Once Bret won the first few rematches subsequent matches didn't do so well and Owen fell from the top of the card, but as a heel he maintained a good position for the next several years. It was really Owen's only singles house show run on top.

To further push him as Bret's top contender, he won the King of the Ring on June 16, 1994 in Baltimore with wins over Tatanka, 1-2-3 Kid and Razor Ramon. The big blow-off was a cage match that went 32:17 and was the best cage match the company ever presented on ppv (until the famous Shawn Michaels-Undertaker match), with Bret winning the first ever event at the newly built United Center in Chicago for SummerSlam on August 24, 1994.

The feud was kept alive to a degree when Owen talked mother Helen into throwing in the towel for Bret, costing him the wwf title at a Survivor Series in November, 1994 in San Antonio. Over the next few years Owen worked mainly as a tag-team wrestler, teaming first with Yokozuna and later with Davey Boy Smith as a championship heel team with Jim Cornette as manager. Cornette was phased out and Bret went heel leading to the Hart Foundation's role in the Canada vs. usa feud in 1997 that turned the company's fortunes completely around and established Steve Austin as a great babyface drawing card.

▶ **They were working a little town in the middle of nowhere British Columbia. Brian Pillman,** a notorious playboy, had a date with some hot babe in Kelowna, where the crew was headquartered for two days. Kelowna was about one hour from the town they were wrestling in. When he got to the house show, Owen told Bob Johnson, a company road agent, to tell Pillman the company had him booked to do a "Say No to Drugs" speech at a local senior citizen's center. Pillman came to do his guest appearance at about 10:30 PM, when everyone was sleeping. Somehow Johnson and the Harts had convinced them to let them give their speech because the elderly people all watched wrestling. Pillman, furious, was telling a group of elderly people in their 70s and 80s about staying away from crack long past their bed time. Owen and Bruce snuck out and drove to Kelowna without him, forcing him to hitchhike back to his hotel. They got into Pillman's room first, put a dog in his bed, grabbed his Badd Company wrestling attire and dressed the dog up in it. They put a bucket of water on top of the bathroom door and unscrewed all the light bulbs. Pillman came to the room furious, as it was past last call and his date, thinking he stood her up, was gone. He kept flipping light switches, stumbled around, got doused with the water when he opened the bathroom door, and jumped on the dog, who freaked out and ran off. There was a joke the next several months whenever they came to Kelowna they would look on the side of the road for a dog running around in Badd Company attire.

OWEN HART VS. DUDE LOVE

Owen was a major singles star from that point forward, with Bret the top heel but missing time with knee surgery. He won the Intercontinental title on April 28, 1997 from Rocky Maivia, before he was simply The Rock. In an infamous incident at SummerSlam on August 3, 1997 in East Rutherford, NJ, he accidentally put Steve Austin's head too low on a tombstone piledriver attempt just before the scheduled finish. Austin was temporarily paralyzed and for a few moments was scared he'd never walk, let alone wrestle again. Hart still managed to unconvincingly pin himself as per the plans, and Austin gained back the title.

After his brother Bret was double-crossed by McMahon in the infamous Survivor Series of 1997 in Montreal, Owen, caught in the middle, went home for a few weeks. One story has it that Owen wanted to get out of the WWF but Vince McMahon wasn't going to let him out of his contract. With Bret gone, Owen would be more valuable as a babyface than before. It was inevitable that he would return and have a big money feud with Shawn Michaels,

and probably be a bigger star than ever.

Hart wound up returning for a great revenge angle for his brother who wasn't there, but the people who double-crossed his brother in real life weren't going to work with him. With no angle, his initial pop faded very quickly. With no program, he turned back heel and joined The Nation for a while to be on the same level with Rock, but Rock had so much more charisma that Hart's star faded as quickly as Rock's climbed. He was floundering, a solid in-ring performer in a world where that mattered less and less. He hooked up with Jeff Jarrett, another wrestler whose career was falling to a similar plight, and the former Debra McMichael, who was really the star of the team, stripping to her bikini or lingerie on PPV.

The other story going around is that Owen was getting ready to retire from wrestling when his contract expired in two years. Certainly, he had told many people that. At the same time, even brother Bruce, who has been around wrestlers all his life, said that every wrestler says two more years, but when the big money is waved in their face, few really walk away. Maybe Owen would have been the exception. Maybe at the age of 36 he would really go home, finish college to get his teaching credentials, get a normal job, have a nice quiet life and get to see his children grow up. Name one wrestler, without the decision forced by injury, who has actually done that.

On that May night in 1999, after a seven minute delay in the broadcast for Hart to be taken out of the ring, Jeff Jarrett and Debra Marshall nee McMichael, who had been working for months with Owen as a tag team combination, were to go on next. Jarrett's back was toward the camera, and when he turned around, you could see something really bad in his face. Fans at home probably figured it was real and it was bad, especially when Debra started crying, but they didn't know how bad. The match went on. The fans were still in a state of shock, not knowing what was and wasn't real.

After a short match, at 8:01 PM Central Time, they inserted the pre-taped feature of Vince going out in the ambulance. Hart was rushed to Truman Memorial Hospital and confirmed dead on arrival. Cause of death: massive internal injuries from a 50-foot fall. Back on television, they went right to a pre-produced video package of the Hunter vs. Rock feud, showing Rock being put in a casket and Hunter smashing the casket into smithereens with a sledge hammer, and later showing Rock backstage out of the casket covered in blood. It was horrifying.

And what does any of this, especially hanging from the ceiling, have to do with wrestling? The answer is that wrestling is what the fans make it.

Three men were on the catwalk at the Kemper Arena at the time of the accident. The WWF hired them from the International Alliance of Theatrical Stage Employees Local 31 to work with WWF officials who had put on that stunt previously. EMTs and the ambulance were at the scene, when normally they are not at WWF events, because they were asked to participate in the angle involving McMahon. Just as they finished the filming and were about to leave, Hart fell and they were called back in.

If there is one thing that is loud and clear, it is the furor of the family, understandable when the brother, son, or favorite uncle dies for absolutely no reason. The disgust in many of their voices over the show continuing leaves no room for misinterpretation.

There was also furor about how Vince handled the situation with Stu. Titan claimed that it didn't announce the death for nearly an hour because they wanted to get through to all the family members. However, Bruce said that it wasn't until 11 PM that evening Mountain time, or two hours after the completion of the show, that anyone from Titan called Stu, and that was Carl DeMarco, President of WWF Canada. Martha was called by Titan almost immediately after the incident. Bruce said he told off DeMarco saying that Vince should have had the guts to call himself. Vince did call ninety minutes later, and Bruce said his conversation about the WWF being their extended family sounded like a promo for wrestling marks.

McMahon taped a television show on Monday in St. Louis as a two-hour tribute to Owen Hart. It was hyped throughout the day in the mainstream media. It featured short quick matches with no angles, all clean finishes, no

OWEN AT AN AUTOGRAPH SHOW SHORTLY BEFORE HE DIED, SEATED WITH DEBRA AND JEFF JARRETT

run-ins, no risque behavior, no hype or storylines, and filled with one wrestler and office personality after another talking in almost reverent terms about Owen. Many visibly broke down. It appeared the vast majority of the wrestlers were sincere and the show was lauded by most who saw it. Virtually all of them talked about his legendary ribbing, how he made working with the company a happier environment, how he spent so little money on the road, and how devoted he was to his family. A few mentioned his in-ring talents. Most wrestlers were totally out of character. Goldust was Dustin Runnels, for example. Jarrett, doing an angle with Debra, talked openly about his own wife and marriage. Mankind talked about how Owen was his kids' favorite wrestler. Mark Henry cried heavily while reading a poem. Certainly the ones who stole the show, so to speak, were Road Dogg, Mankind, Jarrett, Debra, Jim Ross and Jerry Lawler. Shane McMahon spoke for the company as Vince never spoke during the show. Neither Austin nor Rock did speaking tributes, being held off until the very end of the show. With one or two exceptions, almost all of the wrestlers wore black arm bands with Owen or OH on them. On Nitro the same night, Chris Benoit, who broke in with Stampede Wrestling a few months before Owen, also wore the arm band. Though tremendous television, it totally avoided trying to answer the questions of how and why this happened – although admittedly no answer can be sufficient.

Brian Pillman

Brian Pillman's death at age 35 from heart failure was made even harder on his friends and family because it was almost predictable. Many in wrestling, seeing how Pillman had changed over the last year of his life, suspected drug problems. Some over the summer of 1997 predicted he wouldn't be alive at the end of the year. In hindsight, so many knew, but so few did anything, which led to a lot of guilt feelings after it was over.

The official cause of death was heart failure, with cocaine use being listed as a contributing cause. His wife, Melanie, on the ESPN television show "Outside the Lines," theorized that Pillman's use of Human Growth Hormone, which he started taking in the last years of his life because he was a little guy in a big man's sport, may have also played a factor in this heart giving out.

Pillman was found at 1:09 PM Central Time on October 6th, dead on his bed at the Budget-tel Motel in Bloomington, MN. There were several bottles of pills, muscle relaxers and pain killers, all prescription medication, along with one empty beer bottle, found near his body when the police opened the door. No one had seen Pillman since 10:45 PM the previous night and the entire crew was already in St. Louis before anyone knew anything was amiss. There were no illegal drugs found in the room, and the bottles were not empty, nor was there a note. Even though Pillman had his own personal demons, those closest to him believe that taking his own life was the last thing he would ever do. He had relied on pain killers heavily, particularly in the wake of a 1996 humvee wreck that destroyed his ankle. Subsequent reconstructive surgery failed and the ankle did not heal properly, though Pillman tried to hide from nearly everyone just how severe his daily pain was. The truth is, Pillman couldn't even play the field with his local softball team, the "Loose Cannons," let alone compete at a high level athletically in pro wrestling.

This was a double frustration, because he prided himself on his athletic ability in the ring for most of his career and he took his level of performance as seriously as anyone in the profession. He was the prototypical student of pro wrestling. He liked to read whatever he could, and he reacted passionately to it. He watched tapes of old-timers, and loved to talk with them, to learn little forgotten tricks of the trade. When he first went heel, he wanted to see tapes of Buddy Rogers. He read, in fact, memorized the Lou Thesz book *Hooker* in one weekend.

He had wrestled the night previous to his death at the St. Paul Civic Center and was scheduled for a major series of angles continuing his saga with Goldust and Marlena on a PPV that afternoon in St. Louis. According to the story that ran nationally, ref Ed Sharkey at the matches in St. Paul noted that Pillman was sleeping on the floor in the dressing room during the card, which is very unusual. Sharkey said Pillman had a strange look to him. He had a few drinks after the matches with some of the wrestlers and was described as being "tipsy" when he declined invitations to go out to dinner and went back to his room at about 10:45 PM. He left an answering machine message at home to his wife, which is the last anyone heard from him.

The next afternoon, neither Pillman nor Bret Hart had arrived at the Kiel Center in St. Louis as of the mid-afternoon for the evening Badd Blood PPV show. But when Bret arrived and Pillman wasn't with him, the crew in St. Louis became concerned. Pillman had missed two house shows in recent months, one due to an auto accident on the way to a show in early August. His behavior stemming from the pain killers had plenty of people in

PILLMAN IN TOKYO AT THE EGG DOME, IN FRONT OF 66,000 FANS

PILLMAN VS. 2 COLD SCORPIO

the company worried. When they called his house in St. Louis about thirty minutes before the free-for-all was to begin, his wife Melanie didn't know anything. Just minutes later, the police came to her door. Upon hearing the news she fainted. At about the same time, a WWF official called the hotel in Bloomington in which he was staying and was given the news that the police had come and found him dead in his room.

He was in the middle of an angle that was taking advantage of his greatest strength as a performer: his acting ability and his ability to play a convincing version of borderline psychotic. It was an angle that was to result in Marlena leaving Goldust for him. His "loose cannon"

character, created in late 1995, made him the single most talked about performer in the industry in early 1996. It was a character that he took with him almost all the time. His angle, though, blurred the line between work and reality to the point that the wrestlers had no idea where the work ended.

So live, on a PPV, Vince McMahon had to go on with the show moments after one of his greatest fears had become reality, a major star dying on his watch, possibly from drugs. McMahon taped a short cut-in which aired during the pre-game show, and a few times during the broadcast mentioned the death again, in most somber tones. He brought up the presumption at the time that it was from an overdose. As the owner of a company that has had a long and storied history of drug problems and repercussions, his had to be as great a living nightmare as could be possible.

Whatever nightmare he and the company were going through while trying to entertain an audience was minuscule compared to the nightmare of the family left behind. Brian Pillman had a family with five children, with another on the way, which his wife found out just a few days before his death.

Brian Pillman was born May 22, 1962, growing up in Norwood, OH, a working-class suburb of Cincinnati, where the Cincinnati Gardens is located. He was raised mainly by his mother since his father died young. He was born with throat cancer and underwent 31 different operations before the age of three, leaving him with his trademark raspy voice. He wound up being a local high school football hero, but because of his size, wasn't thought to have any potential to play in college. He went to University of Ohio as a walk-on, and not only made the team, but wound up by his senior year in 1983 as a second-team all-American noseguard. As a 5'9" defensive lineman, a combination of weight training and heavy use of steroids bulked him up to nearly 250 pounds. He was bench pressing close to 450 and squatting more than 600 pounds. Still, there wasn't much demand in the NFL for 5'9" defensive linemen and he went undrafted. He went to the Cincinnati Bengals as a free agent, and made the team in 1984, having converted to linebacker but mainly played on the special teams. Although he was not a star, he was popular for being a local product who defied the odds and gained a reputation for being one of the physically and mentally toughest players on the team. As a rookie, he was voted the winner of the Ed Bloch Courage award. He ended up being traded to the Buffalo Bills prior to the 1985 season, but was cut in training camp.

Although Pillman himself may have never been aware of this, the Bills staff had already decided Pillman made the team. But shortly before the final cuts, an assistant coach found his steroids at camp and the team realized he was a little guy all juiced up. He wound up signing with the Calgary Stampeders of the Canadian Football League in 1986, and after playing the first three games of the season, broke his ankle, the same ankle that eventually was destroyed in the humvee wreck, which ended his football career. He turned to wrestling. ▶

Pillman was the 1987 Rookie of the Year in the *Wrestling Observer* poll. He survived the craziness of Calgary wrestling, including suffering a severe shoulder injury that nearly ended his career, and a tricep tear in a very real backstage fight where he was ambushed by a much larger Brick Bronsky. Although he remained good friends with Bruce and Owen Hart, that fight was a wake-up call to him that it was time to leave Stampede Wrestling. He was brought into World Championship Wrestling in the spring of 1989 as a babyface. Pillman

▶ Kim Wood, who was and still is the strength coach with the Cincinnati Bengals, recommended to Pillman that he hook up with the Hart Family and try to break into pro wrestling. Stu Hart used Pillman's stature as a former Stampeder and his wild personality to jump-start his pro wrestling training and rushed him into the ring. He started his career with Stampede Wrestling in the main event of a November 5, 1986 show at the Calgary Stampede Pavilion. With numerous Stampeders in the babyface corner rooting him on, Pillman teamed with Owen and Keith Hart to beat Makhan Singh, Great Gama and Vladimir Krupov. At the time, Stampede Wrestling was developing some of what would turn out to be the biggest stars in the world, including the likes of Owen Hart, Chris Benoit, Jushin Liger and Hiroshi Hase. Another almost unknown piece of wrestling trivia is that during his early Stampede stay, an angle was done where heels attacked his supposed sister Teresa to build to a big match the next week. Teresa, whose real name is Teresa Hays, resurfaced many years later in ECW (Extreme Championship Wrestling) as Beulah McGillicuddy. Bruce Hart and Pillman as the tag team called "Bad Company," clad in sunglasses and leather jackets in the final and most memorable run of Bruce's career, were the territory's top babyface tag team for most of the next two years.

BRIAN DURING HIS INITIAL STINT IN STAMPEDE WRESTLING, A TERRITORY THAT AT THE TIME COVERED BRITISH COLUMBIA, ALBERTA, SASKATCHEWAN AND MONTANA (1987), *FACING PAGE:* PILLMAN FLYING CROSS-BODY AGAINST THE ORIGINAL CUBAN ASSASSIN (1987)

wrestled several television dark matches, but was very nervous and didn't perform well. He gained a reputation for being far more green and inexperienced than he really was. That probably worked in his favor, because once the butterflies wore off and he got his confidence back up, he started having good matches and people thought he was making incredible progress in a short period of time. His first major match with the company was at the 1989 Halloween Havoc PPV show from Philadelphia, where he had one of the best matches on the card. It was more impressive since it was with Lex Luger. The feeling going into the match was that Luger was going to have a hard time carrying Pillman in his first major match. Not so.

Pillman's seven-year WCW (World Championship Wrestling) tenure, largely as a mid-card babyface who was generally considered among the best athletic workers in the company, saw several different rebirths. He was "Flyin' Brian," the heartthrob pretty boy babyface with Tom Zenk, a role he was never comfortable with. He was the personal protege of Ric Flair, including a famous match on WCW Saturday Night that drew what is to this day the largest audience ever to watch that program. He was the high flying lightheavyweight champion having the best matches in the country against Jushin Liger, highlighted by a Christmas week house show run in 1991, and a match-of-the-year candidate on the February 29, 1992 SuperBrawl PPV show in Milwaukee. Based on the Liger matches and his performances as champion, he signed a three-year $225,000 per year contract with Kip Frey, who was at the time running WCW.

When Bill Watts came aboard, Pillman's contract, which by the standards of that time was unusually high for his position as a mid-carder, caused an immediate dispute. Just before then, Pillman's potential really began to show as he turned heel, which was his true calling. Watts gave Pillman an ultimatum: either re-sign a lower contract, or be jobbed out (lose every match so his value as a performer in the fans' eyes would be nil). Pillman refused. After a short period of being jobbed out in the opener nearly every night despite being among the company's hottest workers, he stood firm, claiming he was going to become the highest paid opening match jobber in pro wrestling history until the situation became an

PILLMAN GETTING BACKSTAGE ADVICE AT A WWF EVENT FROM HIS IDOL, TERRY FUNK. *FACING PAGE:* PILLMAN VS. WCW'S BARRY WINDHAM, AT SUPERBRAWL '92

embarrassment for the company. In the wake of all the problems, Watts decided to drop the lightheavyweight division. Pillman's career was back in limbo. ▶

Outside the ring, Pillman's personal life had major ups and downs. He had a well-deserved reputation for being a wildman with an apparently endless supply of beautiful women. He had one girlfriend, Rochelle, who he knew from Cincinnati and lived with in Atlanta, who was viciously stabbed in a break-in while he was on the road. Their break-up years later led to one tragedy after another. The two of them had a daughter, and he also had another daughter from another woman. Rochelle developed a major drug problem and Pillman was far from perfect himself, which caused a child custody battle that turned his and his new family's life into a year-long nightmare. By this time Pillman had married a former Penthouse Pet, Melanie, who had her own background around wrestling. (She was the one-time girlfriend in a stormy relationship with Jim Hellwig when he was riding high as one of the two biggest stars in the wwf.) In

1993, in the middle of the child custody fight, Rochelle was supposed to pick up their daughter Brittany and never showed up. She had disappeared, and nobody, not her family or friends could find her. Pillman became the obvious lead suspect. Drinking heavily and fearful that he was about to be arrested for something he didn't do, Pillman decided to play amateur detective to clear himself. He went to the worst section of Cincinnati, carrying a photo of Rochelle and talked to the corner drug dealers. While he was there, the police were riding by and saw a fairly well-known local celebrity hanging out with drug dealers in the worst part of town. They thought he had swallowed something and arrested him. As it turned out, he had one or two pain killers, and wasn't carrying the prescription on him. He ended up plea bargaining down to a drunk driving offense once he proved he had a prescription for the pills and no other drugs were found. He was still under suspicion in his girlfriend's disappearance, until a few weeks later she was found in Florida, totally messed up, when the car she was in was pulled over by police.

In late 1995, knowing his contract had only a few months remaining and still not receiving much of a

push, he decided to take his career into his own hands, devising one of the more unique approaches in wrestling history. Pillman purposely became, both in the ring and often out of the ring, the "loose cannon." Someone who could and would do anything at any given time. He became a reactionary right-winger on a Cincinnati radio station to get the gimmick over. He continually would do things and say things on live Nitro to seemingly put his position in jeopardy, and his behavior outside the ring around the wrestlers was all part of his work to convince everyone that he had lost his mind. He had seriously talked with friends, most notably Terry Funk who became something of a secret mentor to him, about doing a publicity stunt where he'd run on the field and chain himself to the goal posts during the 1996 Super Bowl game.

Within the company, only Eric Bischoff and booker Kevin Sullivan were aware that what he was doing on Nitro and outside the ring with the boys was work, which is why he stayed on television. The work continued to the point that Pillman had an on-air confrontation with Sullivan, which they worked to look like a match had gotten out of control. The angle was so well done that people believed Sullivan was attempting to rip out Pillman's eye in a fake shoot angle.

So Pillman took his fantasy one step further, in what was billed as a "respect" match on February 11, 1996 in St. Petersburg, where the loser would have to say he respected the winner. Pillman had talked Bischoff and Sullivan into actually firing him, getting TBS to send out the termination notice and everything. At the same time they had worked out a deal with ECW, which was supposed to be the renegade independent group, to slide Pillman over (Pillman largely worked out the deal himself with Paul Heyman and WCW approved it). His appearing on ECW would theoretically give credibility to the fact Pillman really was fired from WCW for whenever his surprise return would take place. Although he never wrestled one match for ECW, nearly every angle and video he did during his brief tenure was memorable. At the same time, Pillman had to undergo another throat operation which would keep him out of action a few weeks. Desperate for ratings in the Monday Night war, WCW ordered Pillman to show up in the audience just a few

A YOUNG PILLMAN WORKS A SLEEPER HOLD ON MAKHAN SINGH, *FACING PAGE:* RIP ROGERS MAY HAVE BRIAN BY THE HAIR, BUT THAT DOESN'T STOP PILLMAN FROM SLAMMING AN ELBOW INTO ROGERS' MIDDLE (1987)

weeks later, and Hulk Hogan, seeing the pop Pillman got, attempted to get Pillman booked onto the heel team in an infamous 2-on-8 match on the Uncensored PPV show on March 24, 1996 in Tupelo, MS. Due to Pillman's throat surgery, his doctor sent a note to WCW saying that he couldn't perform that soon.

Pillman was technically fired from WCW, a worked firing with only Sullivan and Bischoff in on it although by this time the fact it had almost all been an angle was pretty well established. This made him the most talked about wrestler on the inside of the business, and a free agent at the same time. He began negotiating with Vince McMahon, who initially was leery of dealing with him. Pillman, acting completely out of his mind, approached McMahon at the NATPE (National Association of Television Program Executives) convention in Las Vegas. He assured McMahon that everything he'd

done was a work. Ross and Jim Cornette went to bat for Pillman since everyone in wrestling had reservations about him because he was living his gimmick to a scary degree. McMahon decided to start serious negotiations. The original plan was to use the wwf, which at the time wasn't offering guaranteed money, to up his price to Bischoff, figuring Bischoff and Sullivan didn't want to lose the character they helped create. With Pillman just weeks away from his 34th birthday, this next contract signing would be the prime years of his career and he knew the top of the mountain at wcw was blocked with the Hogan clique and with Kevin Nash and Scott Hall arriving. The field in the wwf was more wide open. The basic wcw plan was for him to form his own Four Horsemen with Chris Benoit and two others, and feud with Flair and Anderson once again. It was a good spot, but at that point, he was looking for a shot at the top. With a babyface Shawn Michaels being groomed to be the long-term wwf champion, size wasn't going to be a major issue in being the top heel in that company.

McMahon offered a guaranteed deal, believed to be only the third or fourth time in history he'd done such a thing (although it soon become commonplace given the realities of the wrestling war), which caused Bischoff to up his offer to the $400,000 range. While Pillman was in the catbird seat, just a few days from becoming a real-life hot commodity free agent in the midst of a competitive Monday Night wrestling war, he was still going out of his mind, staying up all night, calling everyone and doing everything at all hours trying to get advice on how to play the game to make the most money. Soon after purchasing a humvee, he apparently fell asleep at the wheel on April 15, went off the road, and got thrown 40 feet into a field where he wound up lying in a pool of his own blood. His face was so swollen that friends who visited him in the hospital couldn't even recognize him. By the end of the week, after surgery which included taking bone from his hip to reconstruct his ankle, he was released from the hospital. Since Pillman had been

PILLMAN VS. JUSHIN THUNDER LIGER, BRIAN PILLMAN WITH THE WCW BELT

orchestrating works on the entire world to keep himself the most talked about name in the industry, many within wrestling thought this was simply the latest chapter of a bizarre work. But this was real. Even though the future of his career in the ring looked questionable, neither Bischoff nor McMahon let up on the offer. Pillman claimed he'd been told he'd recover 100% from the injuries in a few months, although secretly he knew the worst. Eventually Pillman chose McMahon's offer. He thought there was no choice since Bischoff wouldn't eliminate 90-day termination cycles from the contract, and Pillman, fearing the possibility of not being able to return to the ring, didn't want to risk his family's future on what he believed to be a short-term deal.

wwf tried to make a big deal of Pillman's signing, rushing him onto television in a failed attempt to close the ratings gap. Pillman was running around the country trying to keep his gimmick strong while being unable to wrestle. Doing so caused his ankle to not heal properly, and a few months later they had to re-break it, do another reconstructive surgery, and start the procedure from scratch. The ankle fused into a walking position. wwf

created an angle with its top heel at the time, Steve Austin, which positioned Pillman as strongly as possible to explain the injury and an absence while he truly rested and recovered. Just a few days after surgery, in a controversial attempt to establish a new Raw time slot, the WWF did the infamous gun angle where Austin broke into Pillman's house, was held off by a shotgun, and the satellite lost transmission as they teased that shots had been fired. Pillman was largely kept home for the next several months, until he resurfaced doing the announcing on Shotgun to build for his in-ring return after Wrestlemania.

His death unfortunately may not have been a freak occurrence, but a simple end result of an emotional mathematical problem. Although he did defy the odds and numerous medical authorities by coming back and his acting ability was likely to keep him in the forefront as a star for years, his physical limitations had to be driving him crazy. Unlike many who seem to take advantage of injuries while on a guaranteed contract, Pillman felt guilty that he wasn't earning his money during the entire period he was out and felt he had to do whatever the company wanted. WWF officials and some of his business associates were extremely worried about his behavior. Wrestlers who liked him were afraid to travel with him. About five weeks before his death, Ross, who had remained close friends with him and had been counseling him several times per week regarding his problems, ordered him to undergo a drug test. Pillman was furious about being singled out. He had never gone on television so impaired he couldn't perform. Melanie was also worried about the level of pain medication he'd been taking.

He claimed he requested a release from the WWF, feeling he could go back to WCW and slide back into the final slot in the Four Horsemen. His personal situation was rocky for a short period of time, which included him violating a restraining order and Melanie filing for a divorce. After a brief separation, he returned home. He was pulled from the October 3rd house show in Winnipeg and from all Friday night house shows for the next few weeks because of a court-mandated Anger Management Class he had to take for violating the restraining order for four straight Saturday mornings. He went back on the road after the class for the matches in St. Paul and for the final match of his career against Goldust. The drug test came back a few weeks before his death showing nothing in his system except for the prescription pain medication it was well-known he was using. It also showed a small amount of decadurabolin, an anabolic steroid that was very popular among bodybuilders and wrestlers in the '80s. Decadurabolin can stay in the system literally for months. Pillman had apparently used it in a desperate attempt to speed up the healing process for his ankle. Because it was a small amount and the drug has such a long half-life in the system, he wasn't suspended.

Pillman had suffered internal side effects many years before from steroid use in football and early in his wrestling career. He also suffered many muscle pulls and tears which he attributed to his use. This caused him to get off the drugs before it became a major issue in the industry, and he was fairly vocal about their potential problems and the effect they were having on the wrestling business. In fact, when WCW Executive Vice President Kip Frey started doing anti-steroid public service announcements when the industry was under the steroid cloud, Pillman was the first to go on television, admit to prior use and warn others against it.

PILLMAN WITH TOM ZENK

The night after his death, both WCW and WWF opened their Monday night live shows with mentions of Pillman. WCW showed a brief graphic. WWF opened the show with virtually all the wrestlers in attendance coming out for a ten-bell salute. During the show, they promoted an interview with Melanie Pillman, live from the family home in Walton, KY. They showed large framed photos in the family den – of Brian holding his baby son, of Brian and Melanie together and of Pillman and Austin as WCW tag team champions – as teases to build to Melanie's interview. Melanie Pillman had reservations about going on live, but eventually consented. She had a very heartfelt message, a warning for those within the industry to not let her husband's death be in vain. She asked that her husband be remembered as the greatest father in the world and as a warm and compassionate person.

On the afternoon of his death, Rick Rude, legal name Richard Erwin Rood, had taken his eight-year-old son to school, attended a martial arts class and gone out to hit some golf balls. At about 5 PM, his wife returned from shopping and found him on the floor barely breathing. She called 911, and he was revived briefly in the ambulance before going into a coma and suffering cardiac arrest in the hospital. This was April 20, 1999, at the North Fulton Medical Center near his home in Alpharetta, GA, an Atlanta suburb. Rude was 40. He had been working with WCW as an announcer for the Backstage Blast PPV airings of Nitro on DirecTV, and was training for an in-ring comeback after breaking his back in a 1994 match against Sting at the Fukuoka Dome.

The heart attack was determined in an autopsy to have been the result of an overdose of various pain medications.

Rude's death was the sixth death of someone actively participating in the business in 1999. Out of the ring incidents that at one time in this sport and even today in any other sport would have been considered alarming, are now considered regular occurrences.

Richard Rood was born December 7, 1958 and grew up in Robbinsdale, MN. He had a friendship with Curt Hennig from early on, and the two attended high school together. After high school, Rood was working as a bouncer, along with Joe Laurinaitis, Michael Hegstrand (Road Warrior Hawk) and Barry Darsow, at Gramma B's, considered the toughest bar in the Northeastern section of Minneapolis. Even though he was the lightest, he was considered to be the toughest of the bouncers, and was noted for being able to knock people out with an open-handed slap. Years later, he knocked out 400-pound

RUDE HEADLOCKS MASA CHONO IN AN NWA TITLE MATCH

Samoan Paul Neu, who wrestled as P.N. News, in just that way. Tall at 6'4", and very muscular, he was known in particular for having the best abs of anyone in modern wrestling. He had incredible grip strength, and was well-known as a tough street fighter. A noted arm wrestler, he finished sixth in the 1983 world championships in Las Vegas in the light heavyweight division (after placing second in the U.S. nationals in 1980). Eddie Sharkey, who trained Rood, Darsow, The Road Warriors, Nikita Koloff and numerous others for pro wrestling, noted that, "he'd slap guys with an open hand and it looked like their head exploded."

Growing up in Minneapolis in the early '80s, wrestling was part of the local culture with the likes of The Crusher, Verne Gagne, Baron Von Raschke, Bobby Heenan, Mad Dog Vachon, Nick Bockwinkel, Jesse Ventura and later peaking with Hulk Hogan. It was natural for young tough gym rats and bouncers to think about pro wrestling. In 1981, Rood was training for a Tough Man contest under Ray Whebbe Jr., a local figure and promoter who had ties to both the city's boxing and pro wrestling communities. Rood had no money at the time, so he got friends to loan him enough to pay for his training under Sharkey. Because he often barely had enough money for gas to get to his matches, he would sleep in his car. When he eventually became a money player in pro wrestling, he paid everyone back. ▶

It was Jerry Jarrett who made Rood a star. In early 1984, Watts was bringing Bill Dundee in as a booker and he brought in the Rock & Roll Express, Bobby Eaton and Dennis Condrey who formed a tag team called the Midnight Express. In exchange, Watts sent Jarrett a few wrestlers that he had no more use for, Rood, King Kong Bundy and Jim Neidhart being the most notable. With only about one year full-time in the business and never

RICK RUDE WITH HIS MANAGER PAUL JONES IN 1986, *FACING PAGE:* RICK RUDE PUTS THE BEAR HUG ON RODDY PIPER

having been given a serious push, Jarrett changed his name to "Ravishing Rick Rude," and for ring music gave him the popular song "Smooth Operator." At the time Rude wasn't particularly good in the ring, although since most of his main events were against Jerry Lawler, who was an expert at carrying guys, there was no problem having him headline. His interviews weren't polished either, although the potential was there in that he had a great delivery. That and his arrogant personality made people believe he truly hated opponents like Lawler, Austin Idol, Randy Savage and the Fabulous Ones. He had a few traits that made him one of the great heels of his time. He had a unique chiseled physique. A tall and very tough man, he had the confidence and the arro-

gance to go along with it, and he became a natural in displaying those qualities in front of the camera. Rude had memorable programs during a period when Jarrett's business was extremely strong, working as the main heel in the company for several months, managed by Jimmy Hart and frequently teaming with Bundy.

He went next to Florida, under Dory Funk as booker. Rude had a good look, but in a territory based more on in-ring performance, he was usually paired as a tag team with Jesse Barr, a worker Funk really liked and thought was going to be a superstar – almost a Florida version of Jesse Ventura and Adrian Adonis. Still, Rude was put on top as Southern heavyweight champion, with his most notable feud being with Wahoo McDaniel.

His next stop was Texas starting in late 1985, for World Class Championship Wrestling, where he became the first ever WCWA world heavyweight champion. Rude headlined against Bruiser Brody, Chris Adams, and all the Von Erichs during his run in that area which lasted until late 1986. On the biggest show to that point in his career, he worked the semi-main event defending the WCWA title on the May 4, 1986 show in Texas Stadium that drew 24,121 fans paying $193,108. He won via DQ (disqualification) against Brody, in the last true big

▶ **Rood and Hegstrand were being trained by Sharkey to be a tag team. Sharkey invited** Ole Anderson, who was running Georgia Championship Wrestling, Inc., up to his camp to look at his huge students. It was late 1982 and Anderson had just seen the movie "Road Warrior"; he wanted a huge bodybuilder to play the role. He needed a team in a hurry so he flew to Minneapolis, picked Hegstrand and Laurinaitis, using the Road Warriors gimmick. Bill Watts later came up with the idea for the face paint, and the two were immediate sensations. Rood was given a minor push at the beginning. Though he had the attitude that made him a natural heel, he was miscast (because of his looks) as a babyface to feud with then-National heavyweight champion Larry Zbyszko. He didn't last long in Georgia and was sent to work briefly for Jim Crockett in the Carolinas as jobber Ricky Rood, sounding more like a race car driver, and later Watts in the Mid South territory as a good-looking undercard babyface.

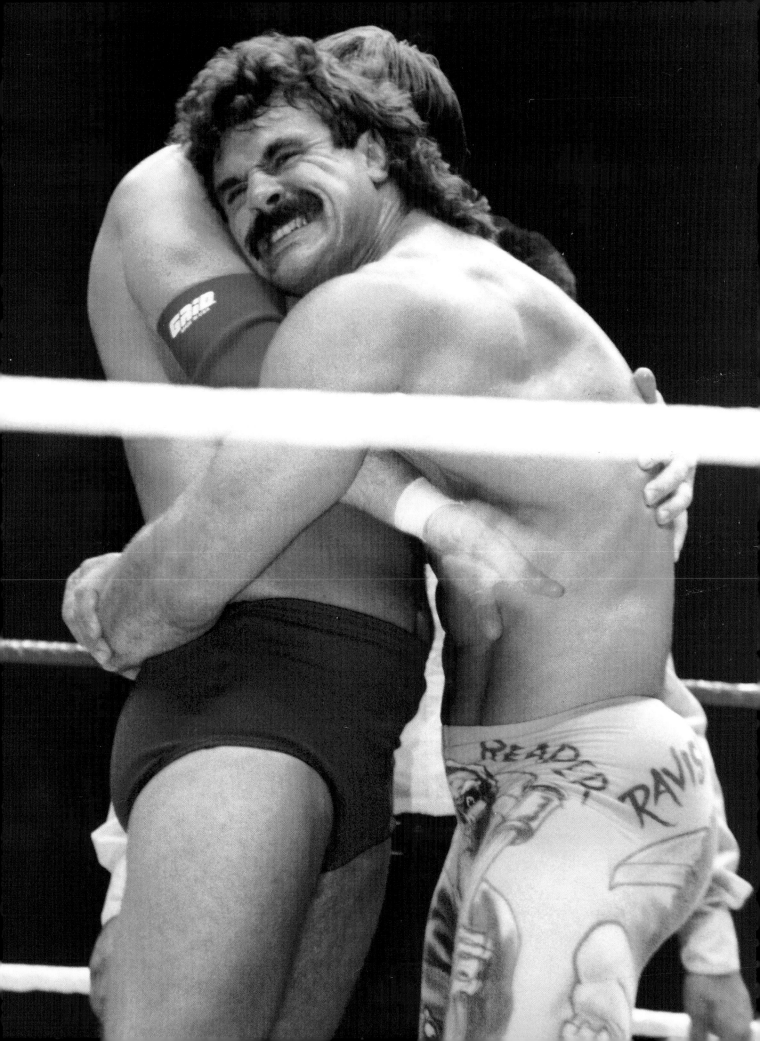

money show in the history of that territory.

Next stop was Jim Crockett's office, which had gotten the TBS contract and was Vince McMahon's only real national competitor during the late '80s. Rude arrived in late 1986, and immediately was programmed as a mid-card heel feuding with old-rival McDaniel. Eventually he was put together as a heel tag team with Manny Fernandez, who had just turned on Dusty Rhodes. Both were managed by Paul Jones. The two spent several months feuding with the Rock & Roll Express over the NWA (National Wrestling Alliance) world tag team titles which Rude and Fernandez quickly won, since the Express was better in the role of chasing the belts than holding them against a heel team that needed to make a reputation. In May of 1987, Rude, without giving notice or dropping the belts, left Crockett Promotions for the World Wrestling Federation at the height of the wrestling war between the two companies. Clumsily, they announced on TBS that Rude had been injured and that Ivan Koloff was replacing him on the championship team. It got even weirder, because about a week later, Fernandez walked out on the promotion as well. Eventually this was settled by JCP airing a taped match from months earlier in Columbia, SC. They announced on television that it had taken place on May 26, 1987 in Spokane, WA (a city JCP wasn't even running) where Rock & Roll Express had won a non-title match taped for a Japanese World Pro Wrestling television show. It was a clumsy scenario since they aired Rude after just announcing he was badly injured and wouldn't be back.

RUDE HAD ONE OF THE MOST CHISELED BODIES THE INDUSTRY EVER SAW, *FACING PAGE:* ONE OF THE MOST CHARISMATIC HEELS OF ALL TIME, RICK RUDE

Although time has erased this from history, Rude was not an instant success in the WWF. WWF was the land of the giants. Rude had a great physique, most notably his long torso and impressive abs, which his pre-match dance highlighted. But he got even more heavily into steroids so that he could match up to most of the main eventers. Because of his naturally thin frame, he was never considered to have enough weight for a program with main man Hulk Hogan, even though he was a stronger heel than most. He was packaged more as a

stripper type. With the swivel hips and the pelvic thrust, he became a human catch phrase a decade before the business revolved around them.

"What I'd like to have right now, is for all you fat, out-of-shape, (insert city) sweathogs to take a look at what a real man is supposed to look like," he'd say as he opened his robe, heavily flexing his arms and abs, generally to thunderous boos. He hit it big with the catch phrase, and with his first program, perhaps also his most memorable, with Jake Roberts, which started when he tried to

hit on Roberts' wife Cheryl in an angle that was years ahead of its time. Even though Roberts pinned Rude every night, Rude's arrogance was such that he continued to get great heat everywhere he went. The feud continued for most of 1988, eventually with Rude being managed by Bobby Heenan. Rude's arrogance in the ring was so convincing that, as great a heel as he was in the territories, every attempt to turn him face fizzled.

Along with Roberts, the other big program of his WWF era was with the Ultimate Warrior. Rude scored one of the first and the few pinfalls on Warrior in his WWF tenure when he won the Intercontinental title on April 2, 1989 at Wrestlemania v in Atlantic City. By this point, Rude had upped his workrate to where he became almost a bumping machine, which led to him being one of the few who could get a good match out of Warrior (about the only others were Savage and Ted DiBiase, two of the best workers of the era). After Warrior had captured the wwf title at Wrestlemania vi from Hulk Hogan at Toronto's Sky Dome, Rude, who had largely feuded with Dusty Rhodes, was elevated to the top of the cards. The storyline was that he was the one who had beaten Warrior for the ic (International Championship) title, climaxing with Warrior winning a cage match in the main event at SummerSlam on August 27, 1990 in Philadelphia before a sellout 19,304 fans and drawing a 3.8 buy rate. As it turned out, this was the only pay-per-view show that he headlined as a single.

His wwf career ended shortly after his SummerSlam main and a dispute with McMahon. While out of action with a torn tricep, the wwf continued to advertise him for a house show run against Warrior in the main events. Rude was the heel challenging for the title in all the advertising in the top arenas. He felt that his name was being used to draw the houses, but McMahon was paying him very little. He wasn't wrestling on those shows, and in the days before significant guaranteed money contracts, injured wrestlers were not well paid until they got back into action. He eventually quit the company over that dispute, and wwf continued to advertise him as a headliner for at least another month.

Rude worked independents and All Japan (where Giant Baba wouldn't allow him to do his pre-match mic work or his stripper dance, but fans did get into the personality he was allowed to show as an acceptable midcarder) until his wwf contract expired on October 27, 1991. He debuted with wcw under a mask as The Halloween Phantom, using the Rude Awakening on Tom Zenk in 1:27 and got the mega-push. Three weeks later, on a televised Clash of the Champions, he captured the U.S. title from Sting due to outside interference from Lex Luger, beginning the last memorable feud of his active career. Over the next two years, he also did very well with New Japan on big shows.

Without question, his career peaked in 1992, when he was the best heel in the entire business and one of its top workers. He headlined numerous house shows against Sting. But just as he really hit his stride as an all-around performer, injuries began breaking him down. Rude mainly feuded with Ricky Steamboat over the U.S. title in early 1992 in matches that were generally considered good but not great. What may have been the best match of his career was on August 12, 1992, at the finals of both the G-1 and nwa world heavyweight title tournament losing to Masahiro Chono in 29:44 before a sellout 11,500 fans at Tokyo Sumo Hall. He is the only foreigner ever to go to the finals of a G-1 tournament. He went through Super Strong Machine (Junji Hirata), Shinya Hashimoto and Kensuke Sasaki to get there.

In late 1992, Rude missed several weeks of work because of two bulging discs. He was never really the same, but by this point his reputation in wrestling was strong enough that it didn't really matter. He was scheduled to win the nwa world heavyweight title from Ric Flair on September 19, 1993 in Houston, tx at the Fall Brawl ppv show in Orlando that summer. Interviews were taped, with Rude holding the belt and talking about upcoming defenses. This was months before the Flair match was actually announced. The nwa Board of Governors were upset at wcw for making the title change without consulting them first, and voted to refuse to allow the change. This led to the final wcw/nwa split. On television, after Rude beat Flair for the same physical belt that had been the nwa world title belt dating back to the mid-80s, it was announced as quickly and quietly as possible that Rude was not the nwa champion. It was stated that wcw International, an organization separate from wcw, had created a world title so this was referred to as the wcw International World title in the United States, and simply the wcw International heavyweight title in Japan.

The final match of Rude's career as an active pro wrestler took place two weeks later. While wrestling Sting at the Fukuoka Dome before 53,500 fans on a show headlined by Antonio Inoki vs. Great Muta, Sting did a running over the top rope dive. Rude caught Sting, but the ringside area was surrounded by a board elevated a foot or so above the ground. In going down catching Sting, Rude's back landed half on the board, blowing out his C-4

RICK RUDE PINS RICKY STEAMBOAT (1992)

and C-5 vertebrae. (Rude blamed Sting for being careless and there was tremendous heat between the two.) Rude got up and won the title with a piledriver and a kneedrop off the top rope after distraction from valet Lady Love (who worked his corner in those days only on Japan tours). Rude never wrestled again and a few weeks later the title change was rescinded and given back to Sting due to the controversy surrounding the finish. Injured, and, in very bitter fashion, Rude was gone from WCW.

"He was 35 years old and in the second year of the biggest contract he ever signed," his wife said. "And then it basically ended. That just killed him. He was a great entertainer and it really hurt him that he couldn't perform."

Rude testified as a very reluctant government witness in the 1994 trial of Vince McMahon and Titan Sports on charges related to steroid distribution. (McMahon was acquitted on charges of conspiring to distribute steroids to his wrestlers.) But aside from testifying, Rude was out of wrestling for the next three years and living in Tampa. Eventually he returned to ECW in 1997 in the role of a television announcer who was there to screw with Shane Douglas, until turning on Tommy Dreamer. At about the same time, WWF hired him to work television tapings as

an "insurance policy" with Shawn Michaels and Hunter Hearst Helmsley in the original incarnation of DX. His rough exterior camouflaged the person who was crazy about his three children, Little Rick, Marissa, and Colton. And he loved to hunt and fish, particularly with Hennig and Rick Steiner.

Friends said Rude had been heavily into Parabolin and Primobolon. At one time in 1998, it was widely rumored he had testicular cancer, which wasn't the case, but he did have a recurring medical problem due to complications from a steroid shot taken in the early '90s while on a WCW tour of England. He had also suffered from phlebitis.

Rude had been attempting to get out of his WCW contract for several months before his death, presumably to wrestle in the WWF. There had been bad blood over the WCW's Eric Bischoff signing Rude from WWF for $300,000 per year on a three-year deal in a notable coup in late 1997. Rude had told friends that he was going to confront Kevin Nash, claiming Nash had also promised him a larger announcing role. Before signing with WCW, Rude had been working WWF without a contract and had been negotiating with Bischoff for weeks for the right time to perform the jump. Rude was brought in originally to be a heel NWO (New World Order) television announcer, however once given the shot, he was clearly not cut out for it. His ECW work, while initially funny, ran out of steam by the second or third week and Paul Heyman kept him in the role just long enough to create an angle to turn him heel and get him out. ▶

When an athlete passes away, particularly one well-known for being heavily into steroids, particularly from heart complications, the discussion of steroids was bound to come into play. In Rude's case, he was 210 pounds off steroids, and while cut, was very thin by the standards of wrestling. He was quite a bit larger during most of his career, particularly his WWF days having to work next to Warrior. The problem with this subject is that virtually every wrestler from that era used steroids. It's rare to overdose on steroids, although if someone is on a heavy cycle, his blood pressure would be raised.

According to friends, Rude had been training intensely for a comeback even though no such deal was specifically on the table. He was in the process of building a new home on 20 acres in Rome, GA, and talked of opening a pro wrestling camp on the property. He had just purchased a new truck. He was about 255 pounds and looking almost as muscular as ever.

Rude's death was covered as a major story every half hour on rotation on the ESPN News Channel along with regularly repeating a segment on deaths of wrestlers, concentrating on Brian Pillman (with an eerie scene of Rude at the 10-bell salute on Raw for Pillman) from the "Outside the Line" show. The same segment aired all day as the cover story on Sports Center. CNN and Headline News also covered it. It garnered a lot of media play in the Atlanta market, and the newspapers in the Twin Cities also ran stories on his death, but there was little other national coverage. Both *Tokyo Sports* and *Nikkan Sports* in Japan ran stories on the death with steroids speculated as a possible cause.

▶ Friends of Rude acknowledge that, at about the time he started trying to get out of his WCW deal, he made contact with the WWF and tried to set up a comeback, pitching them on the idea of a run against Steve Austin. The two were friends and sometimes tag team partners in the early '90s when they were in WCW together as members of the Dangerous Alliance. The hold-up, besides being under contract to WCW, was that he had received a seven-figure settlement from Lloyds of London claiming his 1994 broken back had ended his career as an active wrestler. The settlement, combined with a lawsuit against WCW, was the reason that Rude had worked in a manager/bodyguard/insurance policy role in ECW, WCW and the WWF only on offense, and was not allowed to be put in a position where he would have to take a bump. Rude had attempted to get WCW and the WWF to pay off Lloyds of London on his permanent disability claim which would allow him to return as an active wrestler. Lloyds of London, which will no longer insure pro wrestlers, paid off similar claims to Hennig and Joe Laurinaitis (Road Warrior Animal). Both took several years off and collected on a large disability payment, and both ended up returning to the ring.

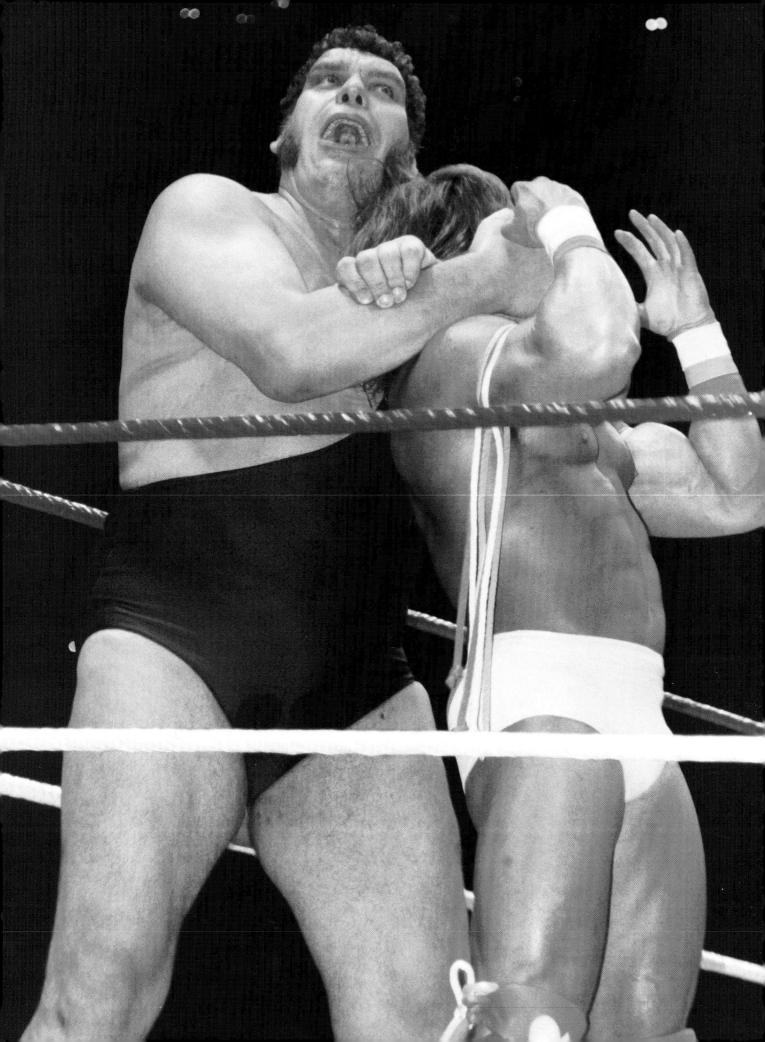

One of the largest men and biggest gate attractions in the history of pro wrestling, André the Giant passed away on January 27, 1993 in his sleep of an apparent heart attack. André, who was 46 at the time of his death, was probably the second most famous pro wrestler on a world wide basis, and correspondingly, probably the second biggest drawing card internationally, in the history of the business.

Known in the business simply as "The Giant," André wrestled professionally for 28 years, and was an international superstar for most of that period. During the '70s, André was undeniably the most famous wrestler in the world, the biggest international box office attraction and the highest paid performer. He was also one of the most recognizable athletes on the planet.

André headlined before what at the time was the largest recorded paid wrestling crowd in history, the 78,000 fans who sold out the Pontiac Silverdome on March 29, 1987 for his Wrestlemania III main event match against Hulk Hogan. The bout was the first million dollar live gate in history ($1,599,000), was the largest closed circuit gate in history ($5,200,000) and set a PPV (pay-per-view) buy rate record. On February 5, 1988, André's rematch with Hulk Hogan from Indianapolis aired on the first live prime-time network wrestling special in the United States in more than 30 years, and the viewing audience, 33 million, made it by far the most viewed pro wrestling match in U.S. history.

Born André René Rousimoff on May 19, 1946 in Grenoble, France, he had a rare glandular disease known as acromegaly. The disease comes from the body's continual oversecretion of growth hormone. It caused him to grow and grow and be one of the world's largest and most powerful men. But once he could no longer grow in height, his body would turn against him. The continual growth would go to his head, his hands and his feet, causing them to thicken and somewhat distort his proportions. He would start aging extremely fast at this point. And it was doubtful he'd ever see his 50th birthday.

In pro wrestling, a world filled with tough guys, the youthful André the Giant was respected not only because he was an amazing athlete for his size, but also because it was well-known in the business that "you don't f— with The Giant." It's really hard to say just how strong or just how tough he was. He was almost never really challenged. But certainly when he first hit his stride in North America around 1973, he may very well have been the most physically intimidating man around.

Already 6'3", André left home at the age of 12. Because of his size, he tried rugby, soccer and even a little boxing, before falling in with a crowd of wrestlers. His first pro match was in France in late 1964, at the age of 18. At the time, he was about 6'7" and 245 pounds, cer-

OCTOBER 1989 – ANDRÉ VS. ULTIMATE WARRIOR, *RIGHT:* **ANDRÉ THE GIANT WITH CHIEF JAY STRONGBOW, MIKE PAPPAS AND VICTOR RIVERA**

Truly illustrative of André's stature — he towers over nwa World Heavyweight champoin Harley Race and Calgary referee Randy Jackson (probably 1977), *bottom:* André's big boot will just about cover Harley Race's chest when it lands (probably 1977), *facing page:* Harley Race goes for a bumpy ride as André body-slams him from the top turnbuckle (probably 1977)

tainly a huge man for his age, but nothing out of the ordinary. How big he wound up will forever be part of the legend of André the Giant.

André left Europe in late 1970 to live in Montreal. Later he moved to a 200-acre estate in Ellerbe, n c where he raised longhorn sheep and quarterhorses. André was known as being 7'4" and 520 pounds. At times, particularly in his later years, the weight figure was probably accurate. Some say his weight was in excess of 550 pounds at the time of his death. But he was not 7'4", or even close to that height. At his tallest, he was probably around 6'10", maybe 6'11". Basketball players who met him generally estimated his height at around 6'9", although because he was proportioned completely differently than any 6'9" man around — with relatively short legs, a long torso and huge head — their estimates could have been deceptive. In 1976, when André had his famous boxer versus wrestler match at Shea Stadium against Chuck Wepner on the undercard of the Muhammad Ali vs. Antonio Inoki fiasco, legitimate sportswriters who took notice of André for the first time estimated him at 6'9", 370 pounds. However, later in his career, André posed in numerous photographs with Shohei "Giant" Baba, and he appeared to be around an inch or two taller than the 6'8" Japanese giant.

In the mid-60s, when André "The Butcher" Rousimoff started wrestling in France, there was no such thing as instant international news or communication. He actually wrestled for about six years before all but the most ardent wrestling fans and promoters in North America were even aware he existed. Edouard Carpentier was always given credit for discovering André as part of the first legendary "worked" story introducing him to fans in Montreal. Carpentier claimed André approached him in France in 1964 and that he went back to France in 1969 and set up bringing André to North America. Carpentier also claimed he told Frank Valois about André after the 1969 meeting at a time when André was already a well-known name in Europe and put the two of them together. By early 1971, American wrestling magazines started showing pictures of this "7'4", 385 pound" superman, who in Montreal was given the ring name Jean Ferre, the always-smiling giant, with little body fat, who could do dropkicks. He went back to the iwe (International

attack Gotch from behind and score the pin to get him into the championship match. Kobayashi won the two out of three fall match, via count out in the third fall.

Jean Ferre, who was billed as "The Eighth Wonder of the World," was an immediate sensation in Montreal. He arrived with the famous Paul Bunyan-like storyline. Carpentier said he was driving around in the French Alps when a huge redwood tree fell in the road. Carpentier, who although only 5'7" was one of the most muscular men of his era, said he tried in vain, but couldn't budge the tree. Suddenly out of the woods came the biggest man he had ever seen, who lifted up the redwood as if it were a twig. Carpentier befriended him and brought him to Montreal to become a wrestler. Carpentier remembered when he first made it big. "André was really living fast," Carpentier said. "As soon as he started making money, he bought a big white Cadillac and drove it all over town. He'd have a stogie (cigar) in his mouth and had women draped all over him. I used to worry about him living so fast but I guess he felt he didn't have a long time to live so he had to make the most of it."

Jean Ferre was usually booked in handicap matches against two men, or in 3-on-2 matches teaming up with Carpentier, who was the most popular wrestler in Montreal. His occasional single matches were limited to the huge heels of the time, who in the Montreal territory were either Killer Kowalski or Don Leo Jonathan. Photos of this huge newcomer who made the giant Kowalski look like a skinny midget hit all the wrestling magazines. News of his box office potential started leaking to the United States promoters when Ferre was booked in his first main event, billed as "The Match of the Century" in the Montreal Forum against Jonathan. The Battle of the Giants with André (billed as 7'4", 385) against Jonathan (billed as 6'9", 320, although he was legitimately closer to 6'5" and 285 at the time) set Canada's indoor wrestling attendance and gate marks with more than 20,000 fans selling out the Forum. Officially, the always-smiling Ferre "lost his temper" for the first time in that match and was disqualified, with every wrestler on the undercard trying in vain to pull his hands off Jonathan's throat, and one swat of the huge paw sending one big wrestler after another flying. The idea was set in stone. He's the nicest guy in the world, but if you get him mad, there is

Wrestling Enterprise) in Japan from March to May of 1971 for the annual Grand Prix tournament which included such luminaries as Billy Robinson, Karl Gotch and Don Leo Jonathan. Rousimoff had a draw with Robinson and wins over Gotch and Jonathan to send him into the finals against Kobayashi. The Gotch match is remembered to this day in Japan, because there was a ref bump, and Gotch picked Rousimoff up in a perfect German suplex but there was no ref to count the fall. André came back to

▶ **The name André the Giant was born in**
1973. The Montreal territory, which had been going great guns behind Ferre, had started to falter because fans didn't believe there was anyone who stood a chance against him. His gimmick drawing power was gone because everyone had seen him for a few years week after week. Frank Valois, a wrestler who had been a major star in France during the '60s, became André's caretaker. Valois represented André and set up a meeting with Vince McMahon Sr. McMahon Sr. changed his name from Jean Ferre to André the Giant and debuted him in Madison Square Garden where he became an immediate sensation. Realizing the mistakes that had been made in booking him in Montreal because of overexposure, McMahon Sr. sent him on the road around the world doing one-night stands, working every territory that was affiliated with the NWA, WWWF and AWA, which in those days meant just about everywhere.

CLASSIC PR PHOTO OF ANDRÉ HOLDING ALOFT 4 WOMEN

nobody and nothing that can physically stop him. During that time, Ferre worked some bigger matches as a special attraction on major AWA (American Wrestling Association) spectaculars, which was actually his first foray into the United States.

Just before meeting with Vince McMahon Sr. and being christened André the Giant, Jean Ferre was given a shot at headlining a few AWA towns in singles matches against that territory's top heel, the ever colorful and controversial Superstar Billy Graham. "I was probably the first person he ever let take him off his feet," remembered Graham about their early meetings. "At the time, nobody ever took him off his feet. It wasn't a planned spot, either. I was holding him in a bearhug and he said, 'Lift me up and take me over to the ropes.' I told him, 'I can't do that.' He just told me to do it. I was amazed at the time he let me. He was a real nice person in that if he liked you, he'd let you do things with him in the ring. I don't believe there was ever anyone in wrestling who could impress you as much by looking at him like André the Giant in his prime. He was a super athlete, for his size, when he was still able to move. For a man that huge, he was a little clumsy, but he was light on his feet. And

he was a great worker in that he never hurt anyone. He'd throw that big punch with that big paw and never threw a potato (a punch that really hurt). His hand was so big but you'd never feel it." ▶

McMahon Sr. booked The Giant during the days when all the major promoters cooperated with one another, and André toured the world, staying a week or two in each territory until the wrestling war broke out in 1984 and Vince McMahon Jr. no longer allowed André to work for any other promotion aside from his New Japan tours. André, on his first go around, was billed as 7'4", 424 pounds of solid muscle and before he'd hit a territory, the promoters would air a photo of him with his long arms outstretched holding up two women with each arm. He was able to easily hold up 300 pounds of weight on each side.

André's life was a series of one-night stands as promoters couldn't get enough of him. His first tour of the territories in 1973–74 as the ever-smiling Giant saw him break attendance records throughout the country. When Eddie Einhorn in the mid-70s challenged the entire wrestling establishment with his ill-fated IWA (Indepen-

ANDRÉ WITH HOCKEY GREAT BOBBY HULL, WHEN THEY PLAYED AS TEAM-MATES AT A CHARITY BASEBALL GAME IN CALGARY, ALBERTA. THE TEAM T-SHIRT DIDN'T COME IN GIANT SIZE! (PROBABLY 1977), *FACING PAGE:* PURE POWER AS ANDRÉ LIFTS MR. HITO AND HOLDS HIM ALOFT BEFORE DUMPING HIM FROM 7 FEET IN THE AIR (PROBABLY 1978)

▶ **André was legendary among wrestlers** for his capacity to drink. Stories of him drinking 50 beers and not having a buzz are legendary. How exaggerated they are is another story. One of the most famous stories was of him drinking 119 bottles of beer in one sitting and passing out in a hotel lobby. Since be was so huge, nobody could move him. They simply put a piano cover over him and let him sleep it off. There are dozens of stories just like that. Wrestlers joke about being out in a bar in the mid-70s with André, and some local wanted to provoke a fight with the wrestlers to prove how tough he was. They laughed about it and signalled for André. Then the local's face turned eight shades of albino and he high-tailed out of the pub.

dent Wrestling Alliance), André was booked in whatever town the IWA would run so the established NWA or WWWF promotion could keep the IWA from getting a foothold. He was the most in-demand wrestler in the world. Every promoter booking a major event wanted André in as the so-called French dressing. The Guinness Book of World Records used to list André as the highest paid wrestler ever with documented earnings of $400,000 in 1974. In later years, when André spent more time working the major Northeastern arenas, his income probably topped the $500,000 mark.

Somewhere along the line, the ever-smiling giant also became the undefeated giant. Wrestling legend has it that he was never pinned until that fateful Pontiac Silverdome match with Hulk Hogan. While not entirely accurate, André did exceedingly few jobs during his career.

Eventually, people no longer wanted to see André laugh through comedy matches with undercard wrestlers and he'd start going into territories to face the top heels. His best drawing matches would be against men who were at least close to his size, with famous feuds against the likes of Big John Studd, Hulk Hogan (when Hogan was a heel not only in his first WWF tour but even earlier in Alabama and Georgia as Terry Boulder and Sterling Golden), Blackjack Mulligan, Killer Khan, Bruiser Brody, Superstar Billy Graham and perhaps his biggest opponent during the '70s, Ernie Ladd, a 6'9", 320 pound former all-pro football lineman who drew many big gates against him in Battles of the Giants.

In the late '70s Valois, who'd been his manager since the '60s, went back home and Frenchy Bernard, a former referee out of Florida, became André's road mate. He lived with him until the time of his death. Valois still received a check from the WWF New York office until McMahon Sr. passed the torch to McMahon Jr. in 1984, at which point he was cut off and lost touch with André. "I never took it personally," Valois said. "He was such a huge attraction at the time. He was a great friend. I lost touch with him in 1985 or 1986. We never had a falling out. Life just took us in different directions." ▶

As the years went by, André got older, then heavier. His weight went to 445, 485 and passed the 500 pound mark. At this point he was far from being solid muscle. Many have said that if André had taken care of himself physically, had gone to the gym, had drunk less, that he could have been the most awesome specimen ever. But it never seemed to interest him.

ANDRÉ VS. HULK HOGAN

Around 1982, Hulk Hogan caught fire in Minneapolis and Japan and surpassed André as the leading draw in the business, and two years later he took André's spot as the most popular and famous wrestler on an international basis. André the Giant and Hulk Hogan wrestled for the first time around 1978 in Dothan, AL at the Houston Farm Center. Hogan was the newest big guy who could be built into an attraction as André's new opponent. Two years later, André participated in the angle which made Hogan a national star. On a WWF taping,

Hogan, then a heel managed by Freddie Blassie, loaded his armpad and busted André's head with a lariat and left him laying. Just before the finish, Hogan lifted André up for a bodyslam. While André had been slammed before, surely no slam in the United States up to that point had been seen by so many people. André and Hogan took their feud to all the major arenas, and not just in the old WWF territory, but across the United States and Canada and into Japan. The first André-Hogan match in New York was at Shea Stadium on August 9, 1980, underneath the Bruno Sammartino vs. Larry Zbyszko cage match main event, which drew 35,771 paid and a record $541,730.

In April of 1986, André got into the ring with Akira Maeda. Maeda was one of the leading stars for the first UWF (Universal Wrestling Federation) in Japan in 1984–85, which worked matches in a so called "shooting-style," and many of its wrestlers, particularly Maeda, decried pro wrestling for not being true sport. The first UWF went out of business at the end of 1985, and Maeda, who had first trained in New Japan, was invited back to the fold. Apparently swallowing his pride because he needed to work, Maeda agreed. It was well-known in those days that Maeda's matches were phenomenal against the Japanese, but largely nothing against Americans. The two got into the ring and whatever spirit of cooperation Maeda had with other Americans wasn't there. André never sold any of Maeda's submissions, and was almost mocking his shooter gimmick. It appeared André kept going for Maeda's eyes. Soon the match had fallen apart and nearly turned into a real fight. André, as immobile as he was by then, was still more than 500 pounds. Maeda got into a fighting stance and started throwing wicked kicks at André's knee. André just stood there, acting like he didn't feel a thing. The few times Maeda got closer and went for a single-leg, André's lack of balance was evident as he went down easily. He wasn't in any kind of condition by this time in his career, so after a few series, he just decided to stay down and dare Maeda to jump on him. Maeda asked one of the older wrestlers if he had permission to finish André off, but the wrestler shook his head no. Antonio Inoki, the promoter, finally jumped into the ring with no explanation and they broke the match up without an ending. André was furious and

ANDRÉ WHIPS FORMER NFL GREAT ERNIE LADD INTO THE ROPES

screamed to Frenchy Bernard, his traveling companion and the referee of the match, that he wanted Maeda back in the ring. Maeda threw his best kick of all after being ordered out, only the opponent was the guard rail.

Just a few weeks earlier, André won the most famous Battle Royal of his career, at Wrestlemania II in Chicago, a match which included a half-dozen NFL football players including William "Refrigerator" Perry, who was coming off a season where he was the most popular player in the league. André got some wire service coverage again – being around the 500 pound mark, he dwarfed the 6'3", 330-pound Fridge. Because the football players weren't workers, they did a dress rehearsal a few days earlier in secret. A few of the wrestlers and footballers were traveling back from the rehearsal when one of the players, Ernie Holmes, a former all-pro with the Pittsburgh Steel-

ers, was bragging about how tough he was. Everyone was getting tired of it but nobody said anything until suddenly André blurted out in that guttural voice, "You talk too much, you know what I mean." Apparently one of the wrestlers whispered to Holmes that you don't know what tough is until you get this guy mad and Holmes didn't say another word the rest of the trip .

It was hardly a stroke of genius to turn André heel in January of 1987 and have him feud with Hogan, which led to Wrestlemania III. André had been a heel for 14 years in Japan. He knew what to do and when to do it as a heel, probably better than in his more familiar U.S. role as a face. He looked the part as well.

Nearly every wrestling attendance and gate record was shattered for the "first" Hogan-André match (Titan went to the extent of actually denying they had ever wrestled previously, let alone had a big money feud spanning many territories). The Silverdome sold out two weeks in advance and it's no exaggeration that, if the building had been large enough, they could have put 125,000 people in the dome that day. By this time, André's physical condition was all but gone. He wore a backbrace underneath his long wrestling tights, and was almost completely immobile. Legend has it that he had total numbness from his knees down whenever he was in the ring.

He was largely kept out of the ring until the rematch on NBC, where he won the WWF title from Hogan with the famous twin Hebner referee finish and then immediately made the famed faux paus of selling "the world tag team title" to Ted DiBiase. He went back on the road working programs as a heel against Studd, Jake Roberts (where he faked a heart attack from fright of the snake) and Ultimate Warrior (where he did the bulk of the total number of jobs of his entire career) and in his last run as a heel, held the tag team title with King Haku, winning and losing the titles to Demolition. He did very lit-

ANDRÉ ADDRESSES THE CROWD IN 1989

tle talking, except when in front of a crowd. Backstage he spent all his time sitting. He was often wheeled to and from his hotel to the car that would take him to the arenas. While in the ring he usually held onto the ropes to keep his balance. He returned as a babyface and did his final U.S. angle being attacked from behind by Earthquake, since he was legitimately going to undergo knee surgery and this would be the wrestling cover reason. However, André never returned for his expected series with Earthquake. The closest he got was an appearance at Summer Slam where he came out as a cripple and the Legion of Doom kept Earthquake and Typhoon from attacking him to set up their tag program. He only made

one more appearance on U.S. television, in Atlanta for the 20th anniversary Clash of the Champions on TBS, walking with two canes.

André never married. He was engaged once in the '70s, but reportedly got cold feet. He had one daughter, although he only saw her once or twice. On January 9 1993, André received word that his father, Boris Rousimoff, who was in his early 80s, was on his deathbed. André flew home to France two days later, and on January 15, his father passed away. André had decided to remain with his family for two more weeks, before he was scheduled to return home. He went to sleep on January 26, 1993, and when his chauffeur showed up the

ANDRÉ "RESTS" HIS HUGE FRAME AGAINST HULK HOGAN DURING THEIR
WRESTLEMANIA 3 BOUT

next morning, André never answered the phone in his hotel room. Finally the staff broke down the door and found him dead. No autopsy was performed so there is no official cause of death, but it is believed he went to sleep and never woke up, dying of heart failure.

The World Wrestling Federation, at its cards on February 1 on the USA network's Monday Night Raw announced the death of André and gave him a ten-bell salute. Fans chanted his name after it was over in some of the cities. All Japan, on its Sunday show in Tokyo's Korakuen Hall, held a similar ceremony. André's death received major news coverage in Montreal, where it ran on page one of the newspaper, and the Associated Press story hit many newspapers throughout the United States. Both CNN and ESPN covered it as part of their sportscast, as did many local news shows on Friday night. All the Japanese sports papers ran major stories as did many newspapers throughout Europe and Australia. Ironically, even though André did the bulk of his wrestling in the United States, his death received far more coverage internationally.

Everyone who ever saw André the Giant will never forget him. Anyone who ever shook that gigantic hand will never forget it. Even the largest men in the world felt small in the grasp of that monster hand. Those memories only made the sight of him toward the end of his career that much sadder.

André's long-time friend and caretaker Frenchy Bernard put together a lavish ceremony in front of 200 to 250 guests on André's 200-acre ranch in Ellerbe, NC, a small town two hours north of Charlotte, on February 24. There were actually very few wrestling personalities in attendance, the most notable of which were Hulk Hogan (who was one of seven who delivered a eulogy), Vince McMahon, Randy Savage, Brutus Beefcake, Rene Goulet, Pat Patterson, Wahoo McDaniel, Fabulous Moolah, Ivan Koloff, and Rita Chatterton. Hogan broke down during the eulogy and was visibly moved from the moment he showed up, breaking kayfabe (an ancient code used by performers and promoters alike in the professional wrestling industry to maintain the illusions vital to its survival in the eyes of the marks) to an extent by saying how André let him slam him in the Pontiac Silverdome in order to take Hogan's career to a new plateau. "I body-slammed him once because he let me do it. He said, 'Slam me, boss.' I'll never forget how kind and how generous he was." Besides Hogan, Frenchy and Jackie Bernard, he was also eulogized by his personal doctor, a ranch hand, a cattleman he did business with and Dr. Terry Todd, a former champion powerlifter who became his good friend while writing a 1981 article on him for Sports Illustrated. Bernard, his wife, and five other riders concluded the funeral by taking André's remains around the ranch for one last tour in a seven horse ceremony. ▶

ONE OF MANY TV GUEST SHOTS, WITH COMEDIANS HENNY YOUNGMAN (LEFT) AND JOEY BISHOP (EARLY TO MID-70S, PHOTOGRAPHER UNKNOWN)

▶ **Getting André to his own funeral was just** another in a series of unique stories. André had asked to be cremated within 48 hours of his death, however there was no crematorium in Paris that could accomodate his size (André was 555 pounds at death). A 300-pound, custom-made oak casket was built for him, but plane flights had to be juggled because the cargo holds on many airplanes weren't large enough to hold the huge casket. When his remains arrived at the Charlotte Airport, the coffin wouldn't fit into a hearse. The funeral home had to bring a forklift to get the 860 pounds of casket and body because it was nearly impossible to pick up. A special mahogany case had to be built for his ashes, which weighed 19 pounds, or about double that of a normal human being.

Bruiser Brody 1946–88

It was the summer of 1988. In Japan, Shohei "Giant" Baba, promoter of All Japan Pro Wrestling, was busy making plans for his biggest card in several years. His concept was for the fans to get involved and pick a "Dream Card." He was pretty sure of what the main event would be: Bruiser Brody vs. Stan Hansen. It would be the first battle of the two most dominant foreign stars of this era in Japan, and it would be sure to sell out whatever building it was booked in.

On the other side of the world, in Puerto Rico, Carlitos Colon who, like Baba, is a famous wrestler and promoter in his native land, was also making plans for his biggest card in recent years. The annual WWC (World Wrestling Council) anniversary show was scheduled for September 10 and was to be the first international wrestling spectacular from a foreign land ever to be shown in the United States. Bruiser Brody was to work the main event.

That afternoon, Barbara Goodish of Boeme, TX, a small town 20 miles from San Antonio, got a phone call from her husband, Frank, better known to wrestling fans as Bruiser Brody. He was on the third day of a four-day stint in Puerto Rico. There was nothing special to report. Since Brody was the James Dean of professional wrestling, a rebel both with and without a cause, she had developed a sixth sense about when things were going to blow up, since they often did. But in this case, all was well. The trip was going fine. He'd be home on Monday and they would have almost a month before it was time for another trip. But Monday never came.

Early the next morning, Bruiser Brody was pronounced dead on an operating table in San Juan. He was the victim of several stab wounds suffered at the hands of

another wrestler in the dressing room the previous night before a card in Juan Lobriel Stadium in Bayamon, nine miles outside of San Juan. The last of the wrestling outlaws had been put down for the count. But this was no angle. And there would be no rematch.

Bruiser Brody was that rare one-of-a-kind performer. He was an enigma in the wrestling business, as much, if not more of a legend in the dressing rooms around the world than he was to millions of wrestling fans on different continents. At 6'5" and 280 pounds, he was one of the leading international superstars in the game throughout the mid '70s and into the '80s. He was the top foreign attraction in both Japan and Puerto Rico. He was the number one star on the independent market in the United States. He was the wildest man in the game. With his shaggy, shoulder-length brown hair and scar-laden forehead, he looked the part as well. He was probably the best brawling-style performer pro wrestling ever produced. In a game where super-heavyweights often steal the spotlight, he may have been the best all-around worker of the 300-pound types in the history of a business which dates back nearly a century. His style, mannerisms and moves have been copied by dozens of wrestlers, spanning every promotion. Videotapes of his matches in Japan were studying material for prospective wrestlers. He was the prototype of how a big man is supposed to work to get over. Every new super-heavyweight that hit Japan, and many in the United States as well, whether consciously or not, copied his repertoire in some fashion, whether it was his crowd-chasing entrance, his moves, his barking, his chain swinging, his licking of his hands during a bloody match, even his walk.

In the United States, however, Brody didn't achieve the fame befitting a wrestler with his marketability, at least not in the post-1984 Wrestlemania era. He wanted to work on his terms. He didn't want to work a taxing full-

POSSIBLY THE BEST BIG MAN WRESTLER EVER, BRUISER BRODY. *FACING PAGE:*
BRODY WAS NO STRANGER TO THE TERM "RED EQUALS GREEN"

time schedule with a major promotion that would threaten to ruin his family life. He was a ruthless businessman. While the wrestling wars had given him a lucrative income, part of the price he paid in return was leaving bits of his forehead in arenas throughout the world.

Frank Goodish was born on June 18, 1946 in Pennsylvania, near Pittsburgh. He grew up in Warren, MI, a lower-class suburb of Detroit. He was aggressive and his size and natural athletic ability made him a football and basketball star in high school. He wasn't easily coached, but he was tougher than anyone else. In basketball, his size and power allowed him to dominate things underneath. While he was good enough for all-league and even an all-state mention, he knew he had no future in it.

Football was his sport. He went to Iowa State University in 1964. His contemporaries remember him as one of the best athletes on the team. But he was wild, undisciplined, and going to class wasn't in his repertoire. He wound up at West Texas State University, an outlaw school in Canyon, TX, near Amarillo, which not-so-coincidentally produced some of the greatest pro wrestlers of this era. As a defensive end, he was strong on toughness and athletic ability, and teammates remember him being amazingly well-conditioned for such a big man. ►

Ironically, there is virtually no record of Frank Goodish at West Texas State University. While his off-the-field hobby of being the champion at racing over a block of parked cars, climbing over each one individually without being out of breath, didn't end his tenure at school, another incident did. One night, apparently drunk, Brody chopped down an important and rare tree on the school campus.

Next came a fling with pro football. He went to the Washington Redskins under Coach Vince Lombardi. He spent 1968 on the taxi squad as a 260-pound defensive lineman with a flat-top haircut before being cut prior to his second season. While he had the athletic ability to play pro football he didn't have either the skills or the discipline to fit into the team mold. He played a bit with the Edmonton Eskimos in Canada, then bounced around semi-pro teams in Fort Worth and San Antonio while working at odd jobs. He also got heavily into powerlifting. While playing for the San Antonio Toros in 1973, at the time the best minor league football team in America, he met pro wrestler Ivan Putski in the gym. Putski convinced him to take the plunge into pro wrestling.

He started under promoter Leroy McGuirk in what later evolved into Bill Watts' Mid South wrestling territory. Several months later he debuted in Texas for Fritz Von Erich, starting with the "fan out of the stands" gimmick. His career took off fast. In late 1975, he got his first major

break as a headliner in Florida, then considered the best wrestling territory in the country, under the ring name Frank "The Hammer" Goodish. He won the Florida State title from Rocky Johnson, father of the Rock, and headlined for several months in a feud with Billy Robinson. The other leading heel in the territory at the time was Killer Kowalski, who convinced Vince McMahon Sr. that Goodish was prime material for World Wide Wrestling Federation main events against then-champion Bruno Sammartino. Brody left Florida for the northeast, where McMahon gave him his new ring name, Bruiser Frank Brody. As a live version of the caveman-turned-powerlifter, weighing around 320 pounds, he was tailor-made for the New York market.

The stay ended with problems after a backstage argument between Brody, McMahon and Gorilla Monsoon, which almost resulted in a brawl between the two behemoths. After that was over, Brody somehow found it impossible to get work in the United States. He drifted off to New Zealand, where he met his wife.

Von Erich brought Brody back to the United States in late 1977. Brody was the perfect opponent for Fritz, the promoter and top babyface in the Dallas area. As a willing bleeder, he sold the concept of Fritz' "Iron Claw" hold to perfection. He had already turned into one of the best working big men around, which allowed him to carry Fritz, who was then in his late 40s. Brody was Fritz' leading rival for years, and held the American title on four occasions in Texas. Fritz repaid him by getting him booked in St. Louis and Kansas City, where he became an instant sensation. Then, with his connections with Giant Baba, Fritz set Brody up for his first Japan tour in January of 1979.

Brody had already caught fire in the United States as one of the five leading box office attractions in the country in 1978. It was pretty well acknowledged that with his size, athletic ability, working ability, gimmick and charisma, he would get over big anywhere he was given even the slightest opportunity. Although Brody's looks made him a natural heel, the fans made it impossible for him to be anything other than a "kick-ass" babyface. He drew many sellout crowds, headlined several circuits at once, and was one of the highest paid wrestlers of the time.

CLASSIC BRUISER BRODY WITH THE NORTH AMERICAN TITLE

Before he ever set foot in Japan, it was established that he would be a superstar. He got a major push, and his philosophy and popularity in Japan changed the business. He came to the ring screaming and swinging a chain. Led Zeppelin's "Immigrant Song" played in the background. The Japanese photographers followed him everywhere and he always had the chain with him, whether it be in restaurants, on the bus, or while shopping. He became an immediate cult favorite.

He was nicknamed "The Intelligent Monster" in Japan. The gimmick of being not only the wildest and most uncontrollable wrestler, but also being a great ring strategist put him on top of the fans' popularity listings. Brody was a favorite of the Japanese press. He spoke slowly, in English they could understand. He was very quotable and knew many of the writers by name. Some of them considered Brody as much a friend as a star wrestler. His face graced countless magazine covers. There were books and photo albums written on him, comic book drawings of him plus all the regular novelties ranging from t-shirts and posters, to matchbox cards and coffee mugs bearing his likeness.

In American promoters' eyes, the stardom in Japan was the worst thing to ever happen to Brody. He was never the easiest wrestler to deal with, but with guaranteed big money coming from Japan, he wasn't going to be held under the thumb of promoters any longer. He was now dealing from a position of power, almost unheard of for wrestlers in that era.

In 1983, Brody took his first major step in raising the ire of promoters all over the country. After the retirement of Sam Muchnick, the legendary promoter in St. Louis, regarded then as being the number one wrestling city in North America, the promotion was being run by a conglomerate of people, among them Verne Gagne, Harley Race, Pat O'Connor, Bob Geigel and Larry Matysik. Matysik broke away from the NWA, used Brody as his main attraction, and for a short while actually outdrew the NWA group. With Brody as important as he was in Japan, especially with Baba in second place in his own bitter promotional war with Antonio Inoki, blacklisting him wasn't possible anymore. After Matysik's group failed and Vince McMahon Jr. began his national expansion, Brody's value to the NWA increased to the point that

A RARE HUMOROUS PICTURE OF BRODY, *FACING PAGE:* BRODY USED WHAT-EVER WEAPON HE COULD FIND, INCLUDING A TOILET SEAT

whatever grudges were held against him were temporarily forgotten in quest of big gates and holding off McMahon.

In the pre-McMahon era, Japan was the spot for big money. Giant Baba and Kanji Inoki (Antonio Inoki's real name) had been rivals dating back to the '60s, and often the business rivalry would explode into all-out war. Inoki was desperate for talent and looking for revenge on Baba as well. A contact was made, and Brody eventually signed a contract with Inoki. It was the most lucrative deal ever signed by a pro wrestler up to that point. For 16 weeks per year in Japan, Brody would earn $14,000 a week in 1985, $16,000 in 1986 and $18,000 in 1987. He also received a six-figure signing bonus.

Brody, in the long run, decided that leaving Baba

was the biggest mistake of his wrestling career. Baba's tours were far more organized and easier on him mentally. Inoki's tours were stressful, with constant pressure on him to do the job. At the same time, with Inoki in need of new foreign talent, Brody acted as the intermediary in wooing Von Erich from his long-time association with Baba, for which he was promised a sizable finder's fee.

At the same time, the biggest thing to hit U.S. wrestling was in its planning stages – Vince McMahon's first Wrestlemania at Madison Square Garden, featuring actor Mr. T in the main event. McMahon's enemies were livid at his nationwide expansion into "their" territories. One promoter actually discussed with Brody, the wildest, toughest and craziest bird in the nest, the idea of going to Madison Square Garden and jumping Mr. T as he came down the aisle, ensuring that McMahon's show would be a flop.

There were at least a few occasions when McMahon and Brody negotiated, but the discussions never got too serious. McMahon certainly knew the money Brody would draw against Hulk Hogan, but perhaps was wary of having Brody – whose reputation was of being something less than a good soldier – in his dressing rooms. Brody was aware of the potential income and exposure from being a major star with Titan, but wasn't willing to sacrifice his independence nor give up time with his wife and son Geoffrey. But if all things had gone as expected, Brody probably would have eventually worked for McMahon.

Brody was there for a number of the tragedies extant in the business. He was in Japan in 1984 when David Von Erich died. One of the most memorable news clippings in the history of wrestling was on Japanese television at Von Erich's Japanese funeral. Brody, with tears streaming down his scarred face, looked down and kissed Von Erich as he laid in the casket. He was the booker for World Class when Mike Von Erich committed suicide, and had a premonition just a week or two beforehand that this would happen. He was also in Texas when Gino Hernandez passed away of an overdose, and was on a tour of Japan when Haru Sonoda went down in a plane crash during his honeymoon.

Brody had been a leading heel in Puerto Rico since his debut in 1983, but in the summer of 1987, he turned baby-

records for the IRS, since he'd been stung a few years earlier and never wanted to go through that again.

Brody, Atlas and Mantell arrived in the babyface locker room at about 7:15 PM for a show that was scheduled for an 8:30 PM start. Most of the babyfaces had already arrived, along with three of the four owners of the business, Colon, Gonzales and Victor Jovica. Quinones was handling the box office. Gonzales was apparently sitting on a bench with a large towel around his right hand. About five minutes later he asked Brody to come into the bathroom for a private meeting, saying, "Brody, mi amigo, come here por favor." This isn't the slightest bit unusual in wrestling circles, as that's where most private meetings take place. About five seconds later, after the door closed, the babyfaces all heard a loud scream and rushed to the bathroom. When the wrestlers opened the door, Brody was holding his guts and blood was spurting everywhere. He was dragged out of the bathroom and panic ensued. Gonzales, whose shirt was covered with blood, left the building. The ring doctor was called to the dressing room. Brody was fully conscious. His blood pressure was normal, however there were air bubbles in his blood, as one of the stab wounds severed the arteries connected to the heart. Another wound, which may have been the fatal one, punctured his liver. His lung was also pierced, possibly from a third wound, possibly by one of the other two. Brody was talking very softly with Colon as he lay on the floor of the dressing room telling Carlos, "No matter what happens, please, take care of my boy."

face by saving Invader #1, whose real name was Jose Huertas Gonzales, from a doubleteam attack by Jason the Terrible and Abdullah the Butcher. The two had been occasional tag team partners over the year before his death.

If there was any trouble brewing, Brody didn't have a scent of it. He had an early dinner with two of the American wrestlers, Dutch Mantell and Tony Atlas who were on the tour in the hotel when a phone call came from Gonzales. He said there were some problems with taxes and he had to discuss it with him before the show. Brody said he wouldn't talk about it with either Gonzales or Colon, and that there was only one person in Puerto Rico he would talk money with, co-owner Victor Quinones. Those close to Brody insist there couldn't have been any problem with taxes because Brody kept immaculate

The card went on as scheduled. The fans, of course, weren't informed as to what happened. The heels weren't, either. Sometime before the card started a message was passed to the heel dressing room which said that Brody had been nicked and wouldn't be wrestling, but he was okay. One of the heels, well-known for exaggerated tales but also considered keenly aware of office maneuvers, said, "Oh my god, Jose killed him." He seemed very distraught, but nobody else in the dressing room took him seriously.

Gonzales returned to the building, wearing a new shirt, and worked his scheduled match that night. Although the promotion knew Brody was in serious condition, they believed he had stabilized. Most seem satisfied the promotion didn't realize just how serious Brody's condition was.

Brody's wife Barbara Goodish was woken late Saturday night by the telephone. She broke her rule of not answering post-midnight calls when Frank was away and was told there had been a terrible accident and that she should come to Puerto Rico right away. Thinking it was a prank she called the hotel and asked for Brody. The hotel clerk already knew the story and put her through instead to Dutch Mantell's room. Mantell, not knowing it was a life or death situation told her it was pretty rough and that Frank might be in hospital for a while.

She packed some things, woke up her and Frank's son Geoffrey, and they headed to Puerto Rico. Abdullah the Butcher met them at the airport and broke the terrible news to them. Doctors couldn't get Brody's blood to clot and stop the bleeding, apparently because Brody had taken several aspirin which thins the blood.

Sunday night, Capitol Sports had a card scheduled for Mayaguez. Word hadn't leaked yet to the public about what happened the previous night, and a sellout crowd was there. Several of the American wrestlers had heard the news and didn't show up for the card. A few left the island almost immediately. Several of the babyfaces went to the police station to give their statements.

Gonzales was arrested the next day on charges of first degree murder and a weapons violation. The alleged murder weapon, a knife, was never recovered by police as it had disappeared from the scene of the crime. Gonzales was indicted on charges of voluntary homicide, but was later acquitted.

While some of the heels claim there had been problems between Brody and Gonzales over finishes during the previous year, nobody could recall any issues during this tour. If there had been serious problems, Brody wouldn't have been caught so unaware. Some claim Gonzales was paranoid about his position as babyface, and Brody was competition for the spot. It is true that the promotion didn't handle the aftermath properly, particularly by allowing Gonzales to wrestle that night.

Gonzales, who claimed self defense, returned to work for Capital Sports shortly after Brody's death. Brody did have a hot temper and was no stranger to incidents in the dressing room, and judging by that alone, self defense can't be ruled out. But that still doesn't answer the question as to why so many witnesses did not testify. It doesn't explain what on the surface looks to be a less than aggressive attempt by the Puerto Rican police to put together the pieces and get at the truth.

After returning home from Puerto Rico, Barbara Goodish received an offer from Baba to come to Japan with her and Brody's son Geoffrey and participate in a Brody Memorial card which took place August 29 in Tokyo. One wrestler who toured for Inoki during late August, when the Brody story was at its peak and Barbara and Geoffrey Goodish had become celebrities in Japan, said the furor was comparable to the response in the U.S. after the death of John Lennon. ▶

▶ **During the service, Geoffrey told his mother,** "I'm not going to embarrass Daddy by crying at his funeral. But when we get back to the hotel room, I think I'm going to have to cry."

Colon's promotion taped its television show the night after Brody's funeral. There was a huge banner on the building wall in Spanish. The English translation was: "We the wrestling fans on Puerto Rico wish to extend our deepest sympathies to the family and friends of Bruiser Brody. Please don't judge the people of Puerto Rico by the actions of one mad man." The banner was filled with signatures of wrestling fans.

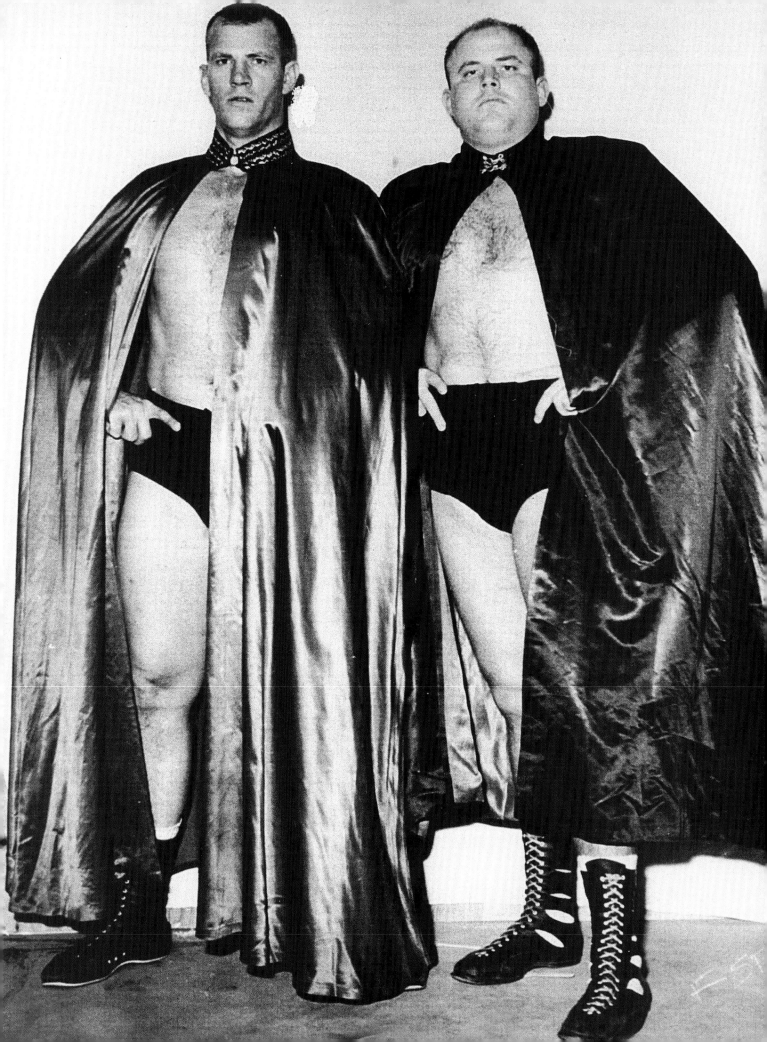

Fritz Von Erich

Jack Adkisson, easily among the most notable figures in the history of this industry, passed away on September 10th 1997 from cancer at the age of 68 at his home in Lake Dallas, TX.

Jack Adkisson was many things and many different people during his lifetime. He was Fritz Von Erich, the monstrous post-World War II Nazi heel with the Iron Claw, one of the biggest stars with arguably the most famous finishing hold of his era. He was Jack Adkisson, a millionaire from the real estate industry who for nearly two decades was one of the leading promoters and most powerful figures in the pro wrestling world. He was the Texas-bred and Texas-fed local hero, the self-promoted toughest man alive, whose "Iron Claw" squeezed the blood and the heart out of every huge villain who crossed his path. He was the patriarch of the ultimate Texas wrestling family.

The Von Erichs were portrayed as clean living and strongly religious. With "off the charts" athletic ability, all of them were going to be world heavyweight champions, a fantasy which exploded into the harshest of realities when his sons felt they couldn't live up their father's promotional image of them. Jack Adkisson was the God-fearing, All-American father who not only was able to sell his promotional fantasy to wrestling fans, but also moved in major religious circles with appearances on the 700 Club.

In 1974, Jack claimed he was deeply moved by a sermon and shortly thereafter a divine voice guided him to open his Bible to Psalms 23. Later, the same force made him pull his car off the road and ponder his sons. He conceptualized his All-American family of wrestling superstars, and to save his family and his dream, became born again.

He was a pioneer in modernizing pro wrestling on

FRITZ VON ERICH (LEFT) AND PARTNER KARL VON SCHOBER IN THEIR TAG TEAM HEYDAY (MID-'50S)

television. He had a unique ability to build up a major wrestling event as a high-class sports spectacular. He set new standards for poor taste that may never be equalled when it comes to promotion of wrestling. Within the state of Texas, and certainly the northern part, he was the single most famous pro wrestling personality of all time. He was large, gruff, athletic, single-minded, had an amazing presence and was domineering over all who were around him. ▶

Before there was Fritz Von Erich, there was the real life Jack Adkisson. He grew up in East Dallas, went on to Southern Methodist University where he was a member of the 1949 football team that included college football legend Doak Walker. Adkisson was only on the team one year, though, because he lost his scholarship during the off-season when he violated team rules and got married. He had a try-out with the old Dallas Texans of the NFL, but failed to make it, and went to Canada to try to continue his football career. He wound up in Edmonton, Alberta, with the Eskimos, and crossed paths with Stu Hart in 1953. At the time Hart was the local wrestling promoter, whose Klondike Wrestling in Edmonton pre-

▶ **Fritz Von Erich's life was, without question, one** of the most incredible, bizarre, freakish roller coaster rides of twists and turns imaginable. Some would say his life was the ultimate proof of karma. But no matter how bad he was, or how good he was, or how huge a star he was as an active wrestler, or how powerful he was behind-the-scenes, one aspect of his life will far outshine all others. He had six children. One, Jackie Jr., died as a child. Five of them, Kevin, David, Kerry, Mike, and Chris, wrestled under the Von Erich name. Four of them died from either drug overdoses or suicide.

dated Stampede Wrestling in Calgary. Hart remembered training Adkisson, a 6'4", 275-pound agile man with huge thighs and small arms, breaking him in along with other future wrestling greats such as Ilio DiPaolo and his later huge rival, Gene Kiniski. Because men who combined size with agility and athletic ability were a rarity in wrestling in the '50s, Adkisson became an almost immediate star and it was only a few years into his career that Fritz Von Erich, master of the "Iron Claw," was born.

No one came close to rivaling Fritz Von Erich's size, presence, big hands, sneer and deadly grip. He would squeeze the temples of his opponent, usually resulting in gruesome blood and submission. He was remembered as the inventor of the face claw, and whether this is true or not, he certainly was responsible for popularizing the move that was later copied by numerous German claw-masters of later generations – from Baron Von Raschke to Killer Karl Krupp, and others like Blackjack Mulligan, Blackjack Lanza and Pak Song. He was already one of the top heels in the country by the late '50s. While wrestling out of Buffalo in 1959, he suffered the first of many family tragedies to come. His oldest son, Jackie Jr., six years old, touched a live wire while he was outside during a storm, was given a major jolt and knocked unconscious. He fell into a puddle and drowned.

It was about the same time that the second member of the Von Erich dynasty came along. Wally Siebe, who wasn't a relative, became younger brother Waldo Von Erich to take advantage of the name Fritz had built. Since Fritz rarely returned East after the death of his first son, Waldo became the Von Erich who was a frequent challenger for WWWF (World Wide Wrestling Federation) champion Bruno Sammartino in the Northeast and was a headliner in the Cleveland and Buffalo areas where Fritz initially made the Von Erich name famous.

In St. Louis, Fritz Von Erich is to this day considered, along with Buddy Rogers and Dick the Bruiser, one of the three biggest drawing heels in the history of the city. He was also a key figure in the re-establishment of pro wrestling as a major draw in Japan in the wake of the death of its biggest star, Rikidozan, in late 1963.

Because the Japanese magazines regularly covered the U.S. scene, top stars like Bruno Sammartino, Kiniski and Bobo Brazil could come to Japan and draw based on photos of them in main events around the United States. Von Erich fit into that category. He was a superstar in the Orient before he ever set foot on Japanese soil because of two victories using his Iron Claw over Antonio Inoki in 1965 in Texas. ▶

In 1966, after just two matches in Japan, Von Erich had surpassed Kiniski, Destroyer, Fred Blassie, Bruno and Bobo as the biggest foreign heel. As famous as Von Erich was to the general public in Japan (largely stemming from his famous match with Giant Baba), it paled in comparison to the term "Iron Claw," which surpassed the vampire teeth of Blassie, the coco-butt of Bobo and the figure four of Destroyer as the most feared maneuver in Japan.

The success of that move may have been the first example of blurred reality in the Von Erich wrestling family. Adkisson was a large, strong man with huge hands and a strong grip. If he really put the claw on a man's temples, with his grip, it hurt like crazy, but it was not a death grip. He used to brag about the power of the claw on his wrestling interviews, and with the demonstrative style and direct voice that made him one of the greatest pro wrestling interviews that ever lived, he was

▶ **It wasn't until November 28, 1966, that Von Erich** came to Japan. His wins over Inoki and reputation from the U.S. set up a natural meeting against the Japanese Wrestling Association's top star, Giant Baba, in Osaka for the International title. Baba won their first meeting via count out, but submitted to the claw in the second fall and was bloodied up by the giant hands. December 3, 1966 at Budokan Hall was the first time pro wrestling ever sold out the venue, and it was also famous for one of the funniest things ever to happen in a major match in Japan. Von Erich used the iron claw, and Baba went to blade his forehead. Baba accidentally scraped the blade across the Von Erich's fingers. Since this match aired live on national television at about 8 PM on a Friday night and drew an incredible rating, the press quickly had to come up with the cover story that Von Erich went into the match with a painful hangnail.

FRITZ VON ERICH WITH 4 OF HIS SONS – MIKE, KEVIN, CHRIS AND KERRY

able to sell himself and the hold. But he also liked to brag about it outside the ring, which had some humorous results. Once in San Antonio on a television show, he bragged about nobody being able to break his hold. The sportscaster, thinking he was playing into the joke, challenged him to put it on, and Von Erich did. The sportscaster responded with a claw of his own, to the testicles, and Fritz, in even greater pain, dropped his grip and limped out of the television studio.

Fritz Von Erich was considered a star of the calibre to be world champion, but never held the NWA title. During the '60s, probably the main deciding factor between himself and Kiniski, a rival with whom he was good friends until the mid-80s, was that the NWA wasn't going to have a world champion with the name of Fritz Von Erich. The title itself was not supposed to be tarnished by a gimmick, such as an obvious fake name or gimmick style performer, not to mention that current champ Lou Thesz would have been far more amicable about doing a job for Kiniski than Von Erich. Sam Muchnick, who was the most influential man in choosing the champion, tried to pave the way for him to become champion years later by revealing his real name as Jack Adkisson. In the early '70s, amidst a major power struggle within the NWA, there was strong consideration given to making Fritz Von Erich a world champion, although he'd use the name Jack Adkisson for NWA title credibility. It never happened, and instead he wound up for a brief period as arguably the most powerful man in the industry.

In August of 1975, Adkisson was named president of the NWA, with the face-saving storyline being that Sam Muchnick was retiring from the position and Adkisson, his long-time friend, was his hand picked successor. Many point to this as the beginning of the end of the NWA. Adkisson was supposed to retire as an active wrestler because of how it would look for the NWA president to be wrestling, particularly under the name of Fritz Von Erich. He decided against it because he felt he needed to keep himself on top, both to protect the business in his territory and to make sure nobody else got over strong enough to fight him for the territory. The president's job had been, among other things, to book the world champion, however with Adkisson wrestling and running his own territory, that job fell into the hands of Jim Barnett, who became

FRITZ VON ERICH

1979 TRADING CARD — FRITZ VON ERICH, *FACING PAGE:* FAMILY PATRIARCH FRITZ VON ERICH WITH PHOTOGRAPHER DR. MIKE LANO (1975)

one of the true power forces in the industry. Adkisson cast the deciding vote in the decision to have Terry Funk beat Jack Brisco and win the title in late 1975, and the world title itself changed at that point. When Muchnick booked the champion, while screw-jobs (matches without a clean finish) and time limit draws were plentiful, the champion always had to win the climactic match in every series against the challenger in order to preserve the idea that, ultimately, the champion was the top man in the business. After Muchnick left, screw-jobs became the order of the day and they became far more creative. The champion won far less often, to the point that the aura of the championship declined as the years went on, even though the belt itself was dominated by great workers such as Terry Funk, Harley Race and Ric Flair. ▶

In 1981, the local Christian broadcasting station began televising Adkisson's shows, and called the show World Class Championship Wrestling which later became the name of the promotion. The shows featured rock music videos, musical ring entrances and production values far ahead of what had been the industry standard. The show started airing outside the territory on CBN stations which started giving the Von Erich kids popularity outside Texas. The huge reactions to the rock ring entrances, which actually had been started five years earlier by Michael Hayes in several other territories, and had been done in big matches in Japan dating back even farther, gave ring introductions a level of heat and began the match with a level of excitement that other promotions couldn't compete with. Soon every wrestler in the country had their own entrance song (Gorgeous George probably started it all in the '40s with his audacious musical entrances).

The kids, David in particular, had already become major draws in St. Louis after Fritz put together an angle in 1979 where then world champion Harley Race juiced and submitted clean in the middle to David's iron claw in a tape that played around the country. His kids got over to the point that whenever any of them faced Ric Flair, they started drawing impressive crowds that on occasion hovered near 10,000. But business was hardly booming the rest of the time. In what was supposed to be his biggest show of 1982, Fritz held his personal retirement match at Texas Stadium on June 14. He beat King Kong Bundy (who had a full head of hair), which drew only 6,000 fans in the 70,000 seat building.

But in one of the legendary angles and feuds in pro wrestling history, on December 25, 1982 at Reunion Arena in Dallas, Terry Gordy slammed the cage door on Kerry Von Erich's head, as he was challenging Flair for the title in a match with Michael Hayes as ref. The match drew 12,000 fans and the first $100,000 gate ever in the state of Texas. It wasn't to be the last. Freebirds vs. Von Erichs was born. The Dallas territory became the hottest in the world and World Class Wrestling became well-known in the more than 60 markets that the tape played in. Nearly every Friday night they sold out the Dallas Sportatorium, and the big shows at Reunion Arena sold out the 17,500-seat building on three occasions that year.

After his son David's death, Fritz built a show around it, the annual "David Von Erich Memorial Parade of Champions." After Mike's death, he had it re-named the "David and Mike" show. A combination of worsening talent and promotion and a lack of taste kept the crowds away. With the promotion on its last legs, Fritz did his final wrestling angle, on a Christmas night show at Reunion Arena, being attacked by several heels and faking his own heart attack. Even the most callous wrestling promoters couldn't believe he'd go to such lengths, particularly since his "condition," updated each week on television, would improve or degrade based on the Friday night house. If they drew a big house, they'd say Fritz was getting better. If the house was down, suddenly Fritz' condition had gotten worse. The angle did revitalize a dying promotion over the short haul, but a few months later, he finally got out of the wrestling business.

World Class Wrestling remained fairly prominent for a few more years, but a bad taste locally began to develop when one depressing incident occurred after another, some in the work, most outside of it. The string of inci-

▶ **Wrestling became a game of every promoter for himself. Moves, such as one to establish** a national television show on cable years before Vince McMahon did such a thing, never got off the ground because nobody wanted television in their markets with wrestlers that they didn't control. In cities like Los Angeles, Atlanta and Detroit in the late '60s and early '70s, when a rival promoter would come into an NWA town, the NWA promoters would send all their top stars into the city for loaded up shows that would knock the upstarts out of the box. By the latter '70s, this happened less and less and promoters fended for themselves, some lost wars or were weakened by non-NWA promoters. By the time Vince McMahon came along and went national in 1984, the once strong alliance was in shambles and was finished off easier than anyone could have imagined.

KEVIN AND DAVID VON ERICH (1979)

dents destroyed the company, each taking the promotional life out of Fritz' spirit. Kerry was busted with drugs in his possession coming across the border from Mexico. The evidence mysteriously disappeared in the police station. Texas promoter Bill Watts, in his attempt to take Mid South Wrestling to a bigger level, hired Fritz' booker, Ken Mantell, who then raided much of Fritz' top talent including The Freebirds and Chris Adams. This resulted in a lawsuit, however Watts was out of the wrestling business before the suit could go to trial. The kids, who were huge celebrities, began ruining their reputations with local promoters and sponsors in their own territory by either showing up incoherent, or no-showing for wrestling and public appearances.

Lance Von Erich was brought in, who looked like a model but couldn't wrestle a lick. Lance, whose real name is Kevin William Vaughn, was billed as the son of Waldo, and thus the first cousin of the boys. However, when Cousin Lance jumped to a rival promotion in Dallas, Fritz went on television and gruffly stated that not only was he not a cousin, but he would also take legal steps to make sure he never used the Von Erich name because he had it trademarked.

In his final years, Fritz largely lived a life alone. His wife Doris divorced him in 1992, blaming him for all the family problems. The only son still alive, Kevin, has been out of the wrestling business for many years now. Neither the WWF nor WCW acknowledged the death of Adkisson on their flagship Monday night television shows, although Dusty Rhodes did mention Fritz Von Erich on WCW Saturday Night, noting that Von Erich had given him his first break in pro wrestling.

Kerry Gene Adkisson was Kerry Von Erich, the Modern Day Warrior. He was one of the greatest athletes in the world. He had the perfect physique. He was nearly unbeatable at wrestling, and in fact, was the uncrowned world champion. He was the second-youngest man ever to hold the most famous and prestigious wrestling belt in the world and he won it from the greatest wrestler of our time in one of the most famous matches the wrestling world had ever seen.

He was loaded with charisma. He'd have gone to the Olympics in the discus if Jimmy Carter hadn't called for the boycott or if some heel hadn't stomped on his shoulder just before the try-outs. He was rich. He had the hottest car. He could literally do no wrong: he was a Von Erich, son of Fritz, the greatest wrestler the world had ever seen, and one of the wealthiest and most influential men in the community. He was born to be a demigod. ▶

Kerry, who was already taking on the dimensions of a bodybuilder, was a high school football star and, like his father, threw the discus. Kerry was both state and junior national champion as a senior in high school, setting a small high school state record that stood for more than a decade. He received a football and track scholarship to the University of Houston. He red-shirted in football but starred in track including winning at the discus in the Texas Relays. But, like his brothers, he only lasted one year in college before pro wrestling came calling.

All three brothers had become national superstars through Adkisson's company, the renamed World Class Championship Wrestling, which was nationally syndicated in 1981 and 1982 through a state-of-the-art television production facility from the Dallas Sportatorium. The first wrestling program preceded TBS and WWF in fast-paced slickly-edited productions, complete with hard rock entrance music. They attracted a largely teenage audience, with a heavy percentage of girls who wanted to see Jack's heartthrob sons. Behind the scenes, bizarre stories of the Von Erichs were legion, largely centered around drug problems.

"I remember going with Gary Hart, Kerry, Kevin, Gino, and David on road trips," recalled Denver sportscaster Steve Harmes. "We'd go to the hotel. David, Kerry, and Gino would load up on Quaaludes and placidyls. They had a doctor who provided them with anything they wanted and as much as they wanted."

Even during the glory years of 1983 and 1984, David and Kerry, who were in huge demand as local celebrities for public appearances, developed bad reputations among local merchants for either showing up incoherent or not showing up at all.

In June of 1983 Kerry was arrested at Dallas/Fort Worth Airport coming back from his honeymoon with wife Cathy in Puerto Vallarta, Mexico. Customs agents found him with 18 unmarked tablets in his right front pocket. He was hiding nearly 300 assorted downers in a

▶ **At about the same time the Adkisson kids were** the high school studs at Lake Dallas High, people remember Jack Adkisson bringing Kevin, David and Kerry to the NWA conventions in Las Vegas, telling the other promoters that his kids would all be future NWA world champions. Kerry, then in 10th grade, was rumored already to be heavily into steroids. The three boys were bonafide high school sports stars and Jack made sure they were constantly mentioned on his television shows, in his programs, in the programs of other influential NWA promoters, and in wrestling magazines.

plastic bag in the crotch of his pants, had 10 grams of marijuana, and 6.5 grams of an unidentified blue and white powder. The incident made the newspapers. The most hardcore Von Erich marks (gullible fans) dismissed the story, believing Kerry's insidious enemy, Freebird Michael Hayes, must have planted the drugs on him. Not so surprisingly, the evidence somehow disappeared from the police station and all charges were dropped.

At Reunion Arena in 1982 more than 10,000 fans came to see Kerry's two out of three fall double disqualification with Ric Flair after which Fritz labeled Kerry the uncrowned world champion. The crowd was filled with high school kids and younger. Most of them had never attended a live wrestling show before and clicked in by relating to 22-year-old Kerry in his chance to win the world heavyweight title for Texas. A rematch was scheduled for a few months later but Kerry's knee went out and he needed minor surgery at the time Flair was booked into Fort Worth. Older brother David took his place and vowed to win the title for Texas. When Flair attacked Kerry and began stomping on his recently operated knee, causing a near riot among the fans, David lost his cool and was disqualified.

The legendary match ended when Terry Gordy slammed the cage door on Kerry's head, a finish imitated many times over the next decade but never with the same results. The resulting Freebirds vs. Von Erichs feud became one of the hottest in pro wrestling history. It also made World Class the first American promotion to capture the quality and set the standard for the wrestling of the future.

From that point forward the Friday night cards at the Sportatorium became weekly sellouts. Spot show business picked up even more with the young, roguish Freebirds as the natural foes. On Thanksgiving night, the loser-leave-town match of Kerry vs. Hayes not only sold out a few days in advance, but thousands of those turned away stayed in the freezing weather outside the arena, watching television monitors through the glass to see what was going on inside.

Then, on February 10, David Von Erich was found dead on the floor of his hotel room. He was 25.

Kerry Von Erich vs. Ric Flair

Kerry, who had teased fans for more than four years with his incredible near-misses in world title matches against both Harley Race and Ric Flair, had promised his fans he'd win the title in memory of his recently deceased brother. Many observers from that time believe that when Kerry was given the title shot at Texas Stadium, it was the first sign that the three-way parity between the brothers was out the window. It was a public sign from either the promotion or the Alliance itself that Kerry was a bigger star than Kevin. Kevin appeared genuinely despondent that he wasn't the one who was going to get to win the title since he was the older brother. ▶

Flair and Kerry rushed through a 13:00 minute match that ended up being the most famous match Kerry would ever be involved in. Kerry won the belt and received one of the most emotional pops in history. At the age of 24, he was the second youngest man ever to hold the world heavyweight wrestling title (Lou Thesz in 1937, at the age of 21, being the youngest). As tears filled the eyes of the fans while Kerry walked down the aisle, his parents Jack (who wrestled his final match that afternoon as the legendary Fritz Von Erich) and Doris met him halfway. Wrestling has never duplicated a scene like that, and may never again. Little did the 32,123 fans, the wrestlers, Kerry or Jack himself realize that, at that moment, when they were on top of the world as the premiere family and promotion in the world, it was actually the beginning of the end.

At the other end of the business deal that resulted in one crowning moment of his wrestling career, Kerry

> ▶**The Dallas area fans didn't notice the** exploitation at the first David Von Erich Memorial Bash on May 6,1984, even with the family photos and David memorabilia being sold at inflated prices, including a recorded single called "Heaven Needed a Champion" cut by one of Jack's gospel singing friends and released literally days after David's death. Exploitation was not on most wrestling fans' minds. After all, in their own world of fantasy, their long-awaited dream had arrived: a Von Erich was about to win the NWA world heavyweight title. Kerry was their man.

KERRY VON ERICH AFTER WINNING THE NWA TITLE

suicide note was found before his body, the promotion announced at a spot show in Lubbock after Mike had disappeared that he was missing and foul play was suspected. The attempt, which didn't succeed, was to work the story once again. The cause of death was an overdose of Placidyl, self administered.

On September 12, 1991, Chris Von Erich shot himself in the head with a 9mm pistol. He was 21. With his brothers gone, Kerry had a big space to fill.

As a performer, Kerry was somewhat green, but carryable, and loaded with a certain jock charisma. At the same time, he wasn't pretty enough to alienate the guys when he started clicking as a draw in 1982. He worked with the best and learned from the best over the next two years until he became one of the best himself. By early 1985, he and Ric Flair toured several territories – Hawaii, Missouri, Mid South and of course his home World Class – and put on state-of-

dropped the title back to Flair on May 24 in Yokosuka, Japan.

While Jack may have deluded himself into believing his sons could do no wrong, apparently his sons believed they couldn't do enough right. Growing up and having to live with the Von Erich name, they apparently believed they had to live up to a standard of athletic and moral perfection that few could attain.

On April 11, 1987, Mike Von Erich left a bar in Denton and was swerving severely while driving home. An officer pulled him over and found a small bottle of marijuana, and two bottles that contained 78 pills of five varieties, mainly painkillers. He was arrested on drunk driving and controlled substance charges. When he was released, it was the last time he was seen alive. While a

the-art matches for that time. World Class television and the Von Erich name were so strong that Flair and Kerry were able to sell out Honolulu for their sixty-minute draw, sell out St. Louis for a sixty-five-minute draw, and draw a $175,000 house at the Superdome in New Orleans, all out of Kerry's home territory, in the first few months of 1985. Most were classics, but not all. One night Flair and Kerry had to work a sixty-minute draw in Fort Worth and nobody could find Kerry. Eventually they found him passed out in his car. They managed to revive him and get him into the ring, but he was zombie-like and Flair had to carry him through perhaps the worst sixty-minute draw of his career. Kerry was brought into Chicago for an AWA card at Comiskey Park that drew more than 20,000, and got a bigger pop than any of the regulars. Every promoter in wrestling wanted to be a part of the Kerry Von Erich gravy train. Still, in early 1986, inexplicably, his performance started wavering.

In June 1986, Kerry was involved in a serious motorcycle accident. He was traveling at an unsafe speed, shoeless and wearing nothing but gym shorts. He made an ill-advised pass and crashed into the back of a patrol car. After 13 hours of microsurgery, they transplanted muscle and skin tissue from Kerry's back to restore circulation and try to save his foot. He also suffered a dislocated hip, a crushed right ankle and many internal injuries. Nearly every specialist put to rest any hopes of his ever coming back to the ring.

The promotion, at this time on a noticeable downslide and feeling the pressure from the expansion of the WWF, Mid South and Jim Crockett's Mid Atlantic Championship Wrestling coming into North Texas, put the big lie back into effect. The Von Erich mythology, as given by Kevin on television, was that Kerry was in a motorcycle accident, but it wasn't serious and he'd be back in the ring in about a month. When that month was up, Kevin would say Kerry would be back in about another month or two. The fear was that, if fans were told it would be a year, maybe more, before Kerry could return, they'd tune out of World Class and either forget wrestling, or turn to the opposition groups which had their own stable of superstars. By Thanksgiving, Kerry showed up on television on crutches and took two baby steps on his own. It seemed well past insanity one month later when it was announced Kerry would return to the ring for a major show in Fort Worth against his former best friend, Brian Adias. On crutches, Kerry came into the building, then, according to a magazine article, a doctor filled a syringe with enough Novocain to numb Secretariat, and Kerry walked to the ring. Basically immobile, he worked a five-minute match, winning of course. But the news was mainly bad. The Von Erich magic was gone in Dallas – Kerry's return drew only 2,326 fans. And in the process, his ankle was rebroken. Four months later, his foot was reportedly fused into a walking position. Miraculously enough, Kerry returned to action on Thanksgiving of 1987 and toured Japan with Kevin a few weeks later. All things considered, the very fact he could still work, let alone at an acceptable level, may have been the thing he should be most admired for. In the fantasy world of his

KERRY VON ERICH

1979 TRADING CARD – KERRY VON ERICH

own promotion, Kerry became a world champion once again. Kerry had beaten Al Perez on March 6, 1988 in Dallas to win the World Class title, since the promotion had split with Crockett, who controlled the NWA title. Kerry traded it once with Jerry Lawler and Tatsumi Fujinami during the year, before the title was done away with after Lawler won a pay-per-view unification match in Chicago.

Somewhere along the way, Kerry's bad foot was amputated. It's not clear whether the microsurgery, failed, or if the operation after his ill-advised comeback match with Adias to fuse the foot was actually the amputation. Most likely it was the latter, since many in wrestling have said that Kerry being in the ring with Adias well before he was ready played a part in his losing his foot. It was largely unknown in wrestling circles, although a few people working for the Dallas office had suspicions since Kerry never removed his boot, even while showering.

KERRY VON ERICH SPENT MUCH OF HIS LIFE IN THE GYM, *FACING PAGE:* KERRY VON ERICH VS. JIMMY GARVIN

The world, or at least the inside wrestling world, first heard the story in the summer of 1988 when he was on an AWA show in Las Vegas against Col. DeBeers. DeBeers grabbed Von Erich by his right boot and suddenly the boot came off, revealing a sock without a foot in it. DeBeers, and the fans at ringside who saw this, were taken aback, and a hush fell over the stunned crowd. Von Erich grabbed his boot, put his leg under the ring to hide it, and put the boot back on. When word leaked about the incident, which initially was only reported in the *Wrestling Observer* and one other publication, denials came from everywhere. Rob Russen, who was doing publicity for the AWA, denied the story despite the fact he was sitting right in front when it happened.

Because of the denials, this turned into one of the most controversial issues of late 1988. The WWF even got involved, before the Lawler-Von Erich pay-per-view match, going to the Illinois commission and trying to get Von Erich banned from wrestling because of an ancient statute in the books about boxers and wrestlers with amputated limbs being unable to perform. The commission avoided the issue by scheduling a hearing for Von Erich after the match date, by which time everything was forgotten – there was no political advantage in blocking Von Erich from wrestling other than hurting the show. The two had an excellent match, with Von Erich losing when the referee stopped the match because he was bleeding. Before the match even started, Kerry was fooling around with the blade backstage and somehow sliced up his arm, which was bleeding as he came to the ring for the match.

In early 1990, WCW called up Kerry to bring him in, thinking they could revive the Flair-Kerry feud and hoping that it still had its box office magic. However, Kerry no-showed for his first scheduled TV appearance and WCW chalked him up as a lost cause. A few months later, WWF came calling and Kerry grabbed the chance to resurrect himself as a national star. Vince McMahon talked Kerry into leaving Texas. Ironically, Brutus Beefcake had just suffered a para-sailing accident and Kerry, now renamed The Texas Tornado, took his place against Mr. Perfect to capture the Intercontinental title at Summer Slam 1990. The reign was short-lived, and Kerry slowly moved his way down the cards. In February of 1992, his father called the WWF and said his son was having drug problems and needed rehab. Kerry had been arrested for forging prescriptions. The much-publicized

KERRY VON ERICH WITH THE NWA TITLE

his indictment, he apparently set out to kill himself. But those who knew him well seem to believe this wasn't a spontaneous decision.

Many of his friends recalled in the few days prior Kerry had come over, seemingly for no reason, hugged them, said "I love you," and then left. Some were confused by his actions. In hindsight, they realized he had been saying his good-byes. His wife Cathy, with whom he had an on-again, off-again relationship over the years, hid all the guns in the house. He said the same strange good-byes to her and her mother and headed to his father's ranch.

As he had done with everyone else he felt close to, when he arrived at 1:30 PM, he hugged his dad and told him he loved him. He borrowed the .44-caliber Magnum handgun he had given his father for Christmas in 1991 and took the jeep saying he needed to find a quiet spot to do some thinking.

About forty-five minutes later, his father got worried. While he was the father of the ultimate fantasy family of athletes, in reality he had already lost four of his six sons. He knew Kerry had to pick up his two daughters, nine-year-old Holly and six-year-old Lacy, from school. He searched his ranch and found that the jeep was empty. Then he found the body partially hidden by a thicket. Apparently Kerry had shot himself in the heart.

Gary Pierson, promoter of the Friday night shows at the Sportatorium, immediately went public hyping a Kerry Von Erich Memorial show for the next evening. Kerry had been scheduled in the main event on the card against Dave Sheldon, who ironically uses the ring name Angel of Death. That afternoon, Kevin Adkisson, 35, the lone living son of Jack, who flew home the day before from a wrestling tour of the Virgin Islands, went to the

drug raid of the WWF dressing room in St. Louis was largely based on a tip that was believed to have been related to Kerry, who no-showed the card since it was during the period Titan had given him for rehab. Kerry finally went through the rehab, and apparently it made a difference over the short run. But by the summer, WWF let Kerry go.

On Wednesday, February 17, 1992 Kerry Von Erich was indicted on cocaine possession charges stemming from a January 13 arrest. He was already serving ten years probation for forging drug prescriptions a year earlier when he was supposed to have been attending rehab. While it was not a guarantee, the odds were very good that his probation would be revoked and he would be sent to prison. When he learned Thursday morning of

▶ **Clinging to the fantasy of the Von Erichs** all the way to the same bitter end that his brothers reached was Kerry's destiny. He was a great athlete, and maybe under different circumstances would have been the biggest star in this profession. But if he had ever reached that spot, the travel and the pressures of the spotlight probably would have caused him to self-destruct. The one thing that as an athlete and as a competitor he deserves the most credit for was being able to come back to the ring with one foot and still perform better than many. But it was the fans that gave him his world, and it was the only real world he knew. It was the world where he was Kerry Von Erich, the Modern Day Warrior.

KERRY VON ERICH SIGNS AUTOGRAPHS AT A CHARITY EVENT — PHOTO TAKEN LESS THAN 2 WEEKS BEFORE HIS DEATH

Dallas media and decried the event, accusing Pierson of trying to capitalize on his brother's death. Many of the 3,038 fans at the Sportatorium sobbed at ringside during the forty-five minute ceremony. Sheldon Simms, Jack's long-time lieutenant in the glory days, David Manning, Chris Adams, Japanese photographer Jimmy Suzuki and Dallas City Councilman Al Lipscomb all delivered eulogies in a ring decorated with flowers and plants, with a huge photo of Kerry, one of his wrestling robes and a pair of his boots on display. ▶

Kerry Adkisson was buried alongside his brothers on February 22 at Grove Hill Memorial Park in East Dallas. Many Dallas area wrestlers attended, although the only out-of-towners there were Jim Hellwig (Ultimate Warrior) and Bret and Owen Hart. Other wrestling personalities in attendance included Scott Putski, Terry Simms, Steven Dane, Calvin Knapp, retired wrestler/referee Bronko Lubich, former referee/booker David Manning, Bob Beddow (promoter in Southeastern Texas), Toni Adams and Jimmy Papa (musician behind the WCW Slam Jam album). Pall bearers included Hellwig, Bill Collville (long-time family bodyguard) and Kerry's ex-father-in-law. There were no speakers at the service.

The Global Wrestling Federation presented a benefit show with all proceeds going into a trust fund for Kerry's two daughters. Promoter Gary Pierson started the trust with a $1,000 donation and Max Andrews, the former television syndicator for the Von Erich's defunct World Class Championship Wrestling promotion, added a $500 donation. Peace was made with Kerry's family as brother Kevin worked the main event and father Fritz made his first appearance at a pro wrestling show in more than two years, and his first at the Sportatorium since he gave up his company to appear in Kevin's corner.

Of the many major deaths in wrestling in recent years, none received as much media coverage as this one. Ironically, neither World Championship Wrestling, which ran a pay-per-view event on Sunday, nor the World Wrestling Federation, which ran its live Monday Night Raw show the following evening, acknowledged the death of the man who not all that many years before was one of the three or four biggest stars in its world. Maybe in that way, Kerry Von Erich did the only thing he had learned, protecting his fantasy world to the bitter end.

Rodney Anoia, who was the heaviest superstar in the history of pro wrestling and a two-time WWF champion under the name Yokozuna, passed away suddenly on October 23, 2000 in a Liverpool, England hotel room a few weeks after his 34th birthday.

Anoia was the most successful of the clan of huge Samoan wrestlers started by Afa and Sika Anoia, his uncles, when they began wrestling in the early '70s. He was one of the biggest stars in the business during his WWF run, which lasted from late 1992 through 1996. ▶

Anoia appeared to have passed away in his sleep from what was believed to have been a heart attack. Reports were that he was drinking heavily the night before. The previous day he had a lengthy phone call from his first cousin, Solofa Fatu, who wrestles as Rikishi, telling him how proud he was of him because he was in the main event for the first time on a pay-per-view. He was on something of a WWF reunion tour, billed as Wrestlemania U.K., built around him as the top attraction. Also on the tour were Greg Valentine, Marty Jannetty and Steve Keirn as Skinner among others.

On the tour, he almost looked like he had mismatched parts. His upper body was considerably smaller than in his WWF days. But from the waist down, he had the hips, butt and thighs that looked like they belonged to a man who weighed 700 pounds.

Anoia was living in Los Angeles as a single father of his two children at the time of his death. The death was doubly tragic to his famous family, which had been devastated earlier that year by the death of Gary Albright in the ring at the age of 36. Albright had married Rodney Anoia's first cousin, Monica Anoia, a few years before. In recent years, Anoia had been living in Las Vegas and was associated with the Buffalo Jim wrestling school. He left

Vegas when that didn't work out. He was not allowed to wrestle in states that licensed wrestlers because his weight was deemed too high a risk factor. The WWF had considered using him, although they were adamant that he get his weight down to 400 pounds, but their hands were tied because they weren't going to sign a wrestler who couldn't perform in more than twenty states, including New York. Still, WCW made a strong offer for him to return in February of 1999, wanting him to do a run-in on the SuperBrawl PPV show, but the deal was never completed and the sides never talked again. In recent years, he had wrestled infrequently on independent shows, including in some states where they ran shows without commission approval, or where the commissions simply weren't aware of his New York suspension. He had also done some international touring. But with his weight ranging

▶ **Whether Rodney Anoia (Yokozuna) was the** heaviest man ever to perform in the world of pro wrestling is a matter of conjecture. It is believed that Anoia weighed close to 800 pounds in late 1996, at about the time the WWF stopped using him because of his weight problem. He was never actually weighed during this period. The Guinness Book of World Records for years listed Happy Humphrey, real name Bill Cobb, who wrestled in the late '50s and early '60s but was never a major star, as the heaviest wrestler of all time at 802 pounds. The belief is that the 800-pound billing, like Haystacks Calhoun at 601 pounds (he was closer to 450 to 500 pounds) and André the Giant at 7'4", was typical pro wrestling exaggeration. There were twin brothers, Billy and Benny McCrary, who wrestled as the McGuire Twins in the early '70s, who legitimately weighed 745 and 765 pounds apiece, and likely still hold the record as the world's heaviest twins.

YOKOZUNA VS. HULK HOGAN

YOKOZUNA WITH HIS BROTHERS BEFORE LEAVING FOR ENGLAND — JUST WEEKS BEFORE HE DIED

▶ One of Anoia's partners in a six man in Mexico was André the Giant and two of their opponents were Badnews Allen and Bam Bam Bigelow at the huge El Toreo de Cuatro Caminos. As legend has it, André went to do his sit down splash, which, due to all his injuries by this point, had become his finisher, on Badnews. Apparently, at the moment of impact, André lost control of his bowels all over Badnews, and worse, due to his physical condition, couldn't get up.

from 600 to 750 pounds, he had been largely immobile in the ring over the last four years of his life.

Anoia was well liked and respected among the wrestlers because, before his weight had gotten out of control, he was very mobile for a man of his size. He was on top for nine months straight as champion, which is still the second longest heel title run (Superstar Billy Graham in the late '70s held it for ten months) in the history of the company. His death was mentioned that night on both Raw, with Vince McMahon calling him the greatest big man in the history of wrestling, and Nitro, where announcers Tony Schiavone, Mark Madden and Stevie Ray said largely the same thing. At first, the decision was made not to mention his name on Nitro since he never worked for wcw, but pressure from the wrestlers who knew him led to the change.

Rodney Anoia was born October 2, 1966 and grew up in San Francisco. As a child, his two uncles, Afa and Sika, had already started in pro wrestling, and Peter Maivia, whose success inspired the clan to get into pro wrestling, was an area headliner. Because of his size and agility, he was trained as a teenager by his uncles and his cousins, Sam Fatu and Samula Anoia who had already started wrestling. He broke in under the name Kokina Anoia, and later, The Great Kokina, while only 18 years of age in the summer of 1985 and already weighing about 400 pounds. The gimmick of the huge Samoan was well established by his other family members, and he played a similar role, working heel in some smaller territories in

Alabama, the wow (an outlaw Alabama promotion) and Continental Wrestling, where he was involved in a short feud with Lord Humongous (Sid Eudy under a mask). He also worked uswa (United States Wrestling Association) for a short period early in his career. He actually became an attraction first internationally, for the uwa (Universal Wrestling Association) in Mexico, when it was a major force where the promotion often relied on bringing giant foreigners in to feud with Canek as its big money program. By the age of 21, he had his first tour with New Japan Pro Wrestling. ▶

Anoia worked in the typical large foreign heel role for New Japan. Since he wasn't a big-name wrestler, he'd usually work in tags on top or in the middle as a single, doing 13 tours between 1988 and 1992. He debuted on the August 1988 tour, and was often used as a monster tag team partner for Big Van Vader, or as the guy who would do the job in headline matches against the Japanese. His first major match was January 31, 1990 teaming with Vader to lose to iwgp (International Wrestling Grand Prix) tag team champions Masa Saito and Shinya Hashimoto. By the summer, they brought his cousin Samula Anoia in as The Wild Samoan to form a regular tag team. On July 19, 1990, the two lost when challenging for the iwgp tag team title against Keiji Muto and Masahiro Chono.

He was in Japan when the gimmick that changed his career surfaced. In 1992, Anoia, then maybe 440 pounds, was introduced to Konishiki, a 580-pound Samoan sumo wrestler who was one of the biggest celebrities in Japan because he was an Ozeki in sumo, which is the position right under Yokozuna. Photos of

YOKOZUNA'S WEIGHT FLUCTUATED BETWEEN 500 AND AS HIGH AS
800 POUNDS

the meeting showed Anoia to be far smaller than the Japanese sumo superstar. The Yokozuna position in sumo is carefully guarded, like entrance into the Hall of Fame in sports. Konishiki was regarded as someone of perhaps Yokozuna level prowess inside the sumo circle, but he had been denied access to such a promotion because of his Samoan/Hawaiian heritage. Only Japanese had been promoted to such a level at that point in the history of sumo, although that is no longer the case. Anoia was getting his first major exposure in the United States during the dying days of the AWA promotion, and was given the name Kokina Maximus, the last name due to the unusually large weight distribution in his gluteus maximus. The meeting with Konishiki led to the creation of Yokozuna, a character based on Konishiki, and perhaps in its own way, to his early demise.

When Vince McMahon brought him in, it was as the ultimate monster heel. He'd be Yokozuna, billed as the greatest Japanese sumo champion, a man who couldn't even be knocked off his feet, which was the trademark of sumos. McMahon wanted him to get much bigger at first, probably to emulate the look of Konishiki, to make him an unbelievably huge monster. He quickly gained weight to well over 500 pounds. Because of all the pressure on the company from the steroid scandal, it was very difficult to bring in monsters, which the company had always liked their top heels to be. Anoia had the ability to get to monstrous proportions, particularly his thighs and butt, which were emphasized in a sumo-like costume, and he could still maintain enough mobility to have a decent match.

Unfortunately, many close to him blame the habits he picked up during the huge weight gain spurt for his death. When the problem got well out of control in 1996 and his weight likely had topped 650 pounds, the WWF

Although he did a Japanese gimmick, Yokozuna was actually Samoan, *facing page:* Yokozuna at his wwf debut with his manager and longtime friend, Mr. Fuji

did take serious action. They attempted to enroll him in a Duke University weight loss program, but he only lasted a weekend, not liking their attempts to change his lifestyle. He rebelled, and wound up returning even heavier. They took him off the road, but kept him under contract, encouraging him to exercise and drop the weight. As his weight appeared to hover around the 750-to-800 pound mark in late 1996, he was being sparingly used, and was eventually dropped from the active roster completely. When they later attempted to bring him back, he failed the New York State Athletic Commission physical, the report saying that his continued wrestling posed a health risk due to weight and heart irregularities. He remained under contract with the company for some time after that.

For his first several months in the wwf in late 1992, Yokozuna, managed by Mr. Fuji, was promoted as the strongest monster heel the company had pushed since the untalented Zeus, coming off the "No Holds Barred" movie, was given a quick push for two gimmick pay-per-view shows. He squashed everyone, never even selling early, then just staggered against higher level opponents, but never going off his feet. It was a wwf gimmick from the distant past. Some 22 years earlier, Bruno Sammartino had drawn two straight crowds of more than 20,000 fans to Madison Square Garden for matches against Crusher Verdu, an untalented wrestler who was never a great success, but had the gimmick that nobody could ever knock him down. The first Sammartino-Verdu match broke a 50-year-old gate record for the building. It wasn't until months later, in likely the last great match of Jim Duggan's career, that Duggan

THE LARGEST MAN IN THE HISTORY OF WRESTLING, YOKOZUNA WAS DIFFI-
CULT TO MOVE AROUND THE RING

actually knocked him off his feet, which led to a major program between the two. Yokozuna was so hot that just a few months after his debut, on January 24, 1993 in Sacramento, CA, he won the Royal Rumble, and was primed to win the WWF championship from Bret Hart at Wrestlemania.

The reign lasted less than one minute. Business was in the toilet during this period. It was during the aftermath of the steroid and sex scandals that broke in early 1992. Many of the company's biggest names, including Hogan, Ultimate Warrior, The Legion of Doom, Davey Boy Smith, and Sid Vicious (as Sid Justice) all left the promotion for a variety of reasons publicly, but there was great pressure on the WWF to clean up the company's steroid problem.

McMahon brought back Hogan, who hadn't wrestled since the previous year's Wrestlemania when he teased a retirement to build up the gate. This was more McMahon wanting Hogan out of the public eye because he was a lightning rod for negative publicity. After Hart lost to Yokozuna in 8:55, Hogan stepped in and pinned

YOKOZUNA VS. OWEN HART

Yokozuna, handing him his first loss in the company, with a legdrop in just 21 seconds.

But business stayed poor with Hogan as champion. McMahon's idea was to build around Hart, giving him the credibility of having been the man Hogan passed the torch to as the young new champion, and keeping Hogan around in the Bruno Sammartino role after Sammartino had dropped the title. Hogan didn't go for being phased out, and because of the big man mind set that was prevalent throughout the '80s in wrestling, he didn't want to

loose to a 235-pound babyface. Instead he picked the much larger Yokozuna to drop the title to at the first King of the Ring PPV event on June 13, 1993 in Dayton, OH, even allowing Yokozuna, after Hogan was blinded by outside interference, to get pinned by his own finisher, the legdrop. The idea was to build up big money rematches with Hogan as challenger, but the gates remained very disappointing and less than two months later Hogan quit the WWF to work in television and continue working major shows with New Japan Pro Wrestling.

Yokozuna became the focal point of the WWF for

about one year as its champion. With Hogan gone, apparently for good this time, McMahon's idea was to create a new Hogan, picking Lex Luger. Yokozuna was billed as the man who defeated Hogan and who nobody could get off his feet. This led to a bodyslam challenge on July 4, 1993 on the USS Entrepid, where the huge foreigner, pushed as the man even Hogan couldn't slam, dared everyone to attempt to take him off his feet and slam him. All the top babyfaces were there and failed. At the last minute, Luger, who had been a heel, performed the slam – not an impressive slam, but a slam nonetheless. Luger was promoted as the new shining star of the company with a bus tour to transform his image. Even Hogan was never given such a major promotion. Nearly everyone expected Luger to win the title at Summer Slam, on August 30, 1993 in Auburn Hills, MI, but instead, in a weak finish, Luger won via count out. The decision was made to hold off the title change until Wrestlemania, but Luger's momentum fizzled when he didn't win the title. He remained popular, but the edge between a top guy and the top guy who means big business wasn't in him any longer.

At the January 22, 1994 Royal Rumble in Providence, RI, Yokozuna beat Undertaker in a casket match when approximately a dozen wrestlers interfered. They basically portrayed Undertaker as having died and gone to heaven, since he was taking nearly a year off for personal reasons. The Royal Rumble was to be a tie between Hart and Luger, leading to Luger eventually beating Yokozuna at Wrestlemania. However, the fan response to Hart was far stronger than to Luger when they were the final two. The WWF hedged its bet, making Wrestlemania into a series of matches on March 20, 1994 in Madison Square Garden, with Yokozuna beating Luger via DQ in the first match, but losing to Hart in 10:38 in a match with Roddy Piper as referee.

Because he had used a Japanese gimmick to become one of pro wrestling's biggest stars, Anoia had received huge publicity and was somewhat controversial back in Japan. The Japanese Sumo Association was upset that someone was using the name Yokozuna, feeling it was inappropriate for an impostor who had never competed in sumo. Nevertheless, the fans had interest in seeing him, but the WWF's May 1994 tour of Japan was a

YOKOZUNA TEAMS WITH THE ORIGINAL DOINK (MATT BORNE), *FACING PAGE:* YOKOZUNA VS. MIL MASCARAS

YOKOZUNA MAIN EVENTS IN FRONT OF A SOLD-OUT BASEBALL STADIUM
IN TIJUANA

resounding flop. The company just didn't understand the market. First, Undertaker beat Yokozuna via count out, and the fans hated the non-finish. Even worse, the next night, against Genichiro Tenryu, the two went to a double count out, which created an even stronger negative reaction in a country where fans had grown to expect all matches to have clean finishes. On the final night of the tour, in a title match against Hart, Yokozuna lost via DQ due to outside interference from Mr. Fuji, leading to a similar reaction.

By the fall, he feuded with Undertaker in his comeback matches, but those were poor draws. That, combined with his lack of stamina and mobility to work singles matches, led to pairing him with Owen Hart, a great worker, in a tag team with Jim Cornette as the mouthpiece. The two won the WWF tag titles from The Smoking Gunns (Billy and Bart Gunn, the latter now All Japan's Mike Barton) at Wrestlemania XI on April 2, 1995 in Hartford. At the King of the Ring PPV on June 25, 1995, he lost in the first match of the show via count out to Savio Vega. They dropped the belts on September 25, 1995 at Raw in Grand Rapids, MI back to the Smoking Gunns.

His contract was running out in early 1996 as he was being phased down the cards. Hogan, never having gotten his win back from the Dayton match, made a big play to bring him into WCW for that purpose, just as he later did with Ultimate Warrior, the other wrestler he had never gotten his win back from in the WWF. A play was made to bring the entire Samoan clan in, with Afa (who had been friends with Hogan dating back to the late '70s), Yokozuna, and Fatu (whose contract was also expiring). McMahon got wind of it, and before Scott Hall and Kevin Nash made themselves into bigger stars and turned WCW around with their jump, McMahon offered Yokozuna and Fatu major pushes as singles babyfaces. They were given roles, but neither got over and the big pushes never materialized. Yokozuna feuded with Cornette's stable of Vader, Hart and Davey Boy Smith, but it was more his role to put Vader over. By the end of the summer, he was no longer a factor due to his weight. He lost to Steve Austin at the SummerSlam PPV just 1:52 into in a match where they gimmicked the ropes collapsing under his weight. His final appearance in the WWF was in Madison Square Garden at Survivor Series on November 17, 1996 in a throwaway match teaming with Flash Funk (Too Cold Scorpio), Jimmy Snuka and Vega losing to Faarooq, Vader, the new Razor Ramon (Rick Bogner) and the new Diesel (Glen Jacobs, now Kane). The match ended with everyone in the match disqualified at once. Yokozuna may have been 800 pounds by this point and could do almost nothing in the ring. At the age of 30, his career, for all interests and purposes, was over.

He was eventually released by the WWF in 1997 due to weight problems. He wrestled on rare occasions on indie shows. His last major appearance was one many would rather forget, the embarrassing main event at the October 10, 1999 Heroes of Wrestling PPV from St. Louis, MS where he, looking to be about 600 pounds, teamed with Jake Roberts, putting over King Kong Bundy and Jim Neidhart.

YOKOZUNA BACKSTAGE WITH FAMOUS MEXICAN WRESTLING/LUCHA STAR-WARS/AZTEC TV STAR MASCOT, ALUSHE

Who dat think they can beat dat Dog? Who dat?

The old Downtown Municipal Auditorium in New Orleans every Monday night was known as The Dog's Yard. It was a wild and dangerous scene. It was in a part of town that the people from the suburbs knew to avoid, and the scene inside the building exemplified exactly what they were afraid of. There were usually some 5,000 to 8,000 fans packing the place. There were near and occasionally outright riots practicaly every week in the building. Sometimes there were riots in the streets outside by fans who were turned away at the door the night there were sellouts. The security force was aggressive and legendary, and on more than one occasion it literally saved the lives of the heels that were threatening their king. His opponents often wouldn't even dare drive to the building for fear their cars would be destroyed, and would sneak out of the arena in the trunk of someone else's car so as not to be followed by the dangerous mob. The crowd was heavily African-American. Black was the term in those days. Their king was the Junkyard Dog.

From 1980 to 1984, The Dog barked, danced and head-butted his way through opponents fed to him while the fans in the Big Easy created the chant and repeated it every Monday night: "Who dat think they can beat dat Dog? Who dat?" The fans came to see the Dog thump foe after foe with his powerslam, but along the way, Sylvester Ritter had real-life opponents who had the power to put him down for the three count. Nobody is really sure which came first, the marital problems or the cocaine, but they were a devastating one-two punch that was chipping away at the armor of the Junkyard Dog.

On a national basis, the Junkyard Dog will best be

CLASSIC JUNKYARD DOG THUMP

known for his run in the World Wrestling Federation from late 1984 to 1987 when he was a headliner and one of the top babyfaces. It was an era that will go down as being known for cartoon wrestling, network television exposure, steroids, the beginnings of Wrestlemania, the birth of toy action figures and the infancy of pay-per-view television. He was on the first Wrestlemania, beating Greg Valentine via count out in a match for Valentine's Intercontinental title. He was on the first Saturday Night Main Event on NBC six weeks later. He won the first and only Wrestling Classic PPV tournament in Chicago. He was in the final match in early 1986 when NBC set the all-time ratings record in the 11:30 PM time slot, teaming with Ricky Steamboat to beat Don Muraco and Mr. Fuji. He was actually in the best match at the second Wrestlemania, teaming with Tito Santana to lose to Dory and Terry Funk, and one month later on NBC teamed with Hogan to gain revenge on the Funks. He beat Adrian Adonis via count out in one of the top matches before 69,300 fans in Toronto underneath the Hulk Hogan vs. Paul Orndorff match on August 8, 1986, and his run as one of the main stars ended when he lost to Harley Race at the most famous Wrestlemania of them all, on March 29, 1987 at the Pontiac Silverdome. He lost his job shortly thereafter and despite a few comebacks, he really could no longer be pushed as a major star.

But the Junkyard Dog that those closest to him remember was the one who set New Orleans, and the rest of Louisiana, Mississippi, Oklahoma, Arkansas and parts of Texas on fire several years earlier when the wrestling world was a very different place.

Within his domain, the Junkyard Dog was one of the most genuinely loved pro wrestling personalities in any region at any time. It was a rare part of wrestling history, when all the dots connect at once and the fantasy actually

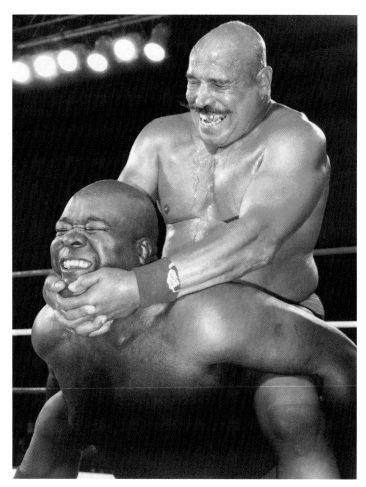

IRON SHEIK HAS JUNKYARD DOG IN A CAMEL CLUTCH IN A WWF MATCH,
FACING PAGE: JUNKYARD DOG HITS IRON SHEIK WITH HIS OWN IRANIAN FLAG

becomes highly-charged emotional reality to a number of people. It was only a fleeting time, a few years of record business in cities where the population wasn't all that large and the economy was all that poor. Bill Watts, the promoter and behind-the-scenes architect of his success, called the period "Camelot." Of course, that fantasy in hindsight was certainly different from the reality of the boys – working seven days a week, often twice on Saturdays and Sundays, driving upwards of 2,000 miles per week on two-lane roads winding around several states. It was a period that gave you constant headaches, nightmares and fears while it was going on, but one that molded all those who lived it into wrestling minds that understood concepts of the business and television that few since that time have really grasped. It put all of them way ahead of the pack for years to come.

The death of Junkyard Dog closed the door on the hottest era ever for pro wrestling in that part of the country – all the monster crowds, and television ratings

that would literally boggle the mind, like 50 shares on UHF stations. Realistically, had it not been for the drugs, had he been as motivated as some of his contemporaries whose careers stood the test of time, and had he maintained his conditioning, he very likely could have still been a top star today. He might have had the kind of historical run that people like The Crusher and Dick the Bruiser had in their home cities, where they could still headline at the age of 50, in the same class of wrestlers like Ric Flair, Roddy Piper, Hulk Hogan and Randy Savage.

Sylvester Ritter died on June 2, 1998 when he rolled his car three times after apparently falling asleep at the wheel, while driving back to his home in Mississippi from where he grew up in Wadesboro, NC. He was 45 years old. The company that made him a superstar and that he made millions of dollars for, Mid South Wrestling, had passed away 11 years before. In a wrestling sense, the Junkyard Dog died several years earlier, as well. He was a long forgotten name out of pro wrestling nostalgia at his death, even though many of his contemporaries are still around.

The most famous native son of Wadesboro, a poor, rural, heavily black city off the beaten path from Charlotte, was a football and wrestling star at Bowman High School, graduating in 1971. He was actually a good enough offensive guard at Fayetteville State University to be drafted in the 12th round by the Houston Oilers in 1975 after graduating with a B.A. in History and Political Science. And as everyone who knew him in his prime in the Mid South would attest, contrary to his WWF role, the Dog was no dummy, with a quick-wit and a classic interview style that was largely responsible for creating his weekly magic.

He was cut by the Oilers after blowing out his knee and the next season tried out for the Green Bay Packers, but was again cut in camp. He was living in Charlotte, working as a deputy sheriff for Mecklenburg County when they had a wrestling tournament among the big tough members of the department. Many of them were as big as he was, and he was strong enough to throw everyone around. One of the deputies worked part-time as a referee for Pedro Martinez and suggested to Ritter that he try pro wrestling. Martinez was running a dying outlaw promotion called the IWA (Independent Wrestling Alliance) against Jim Crockett Jr. in the area,

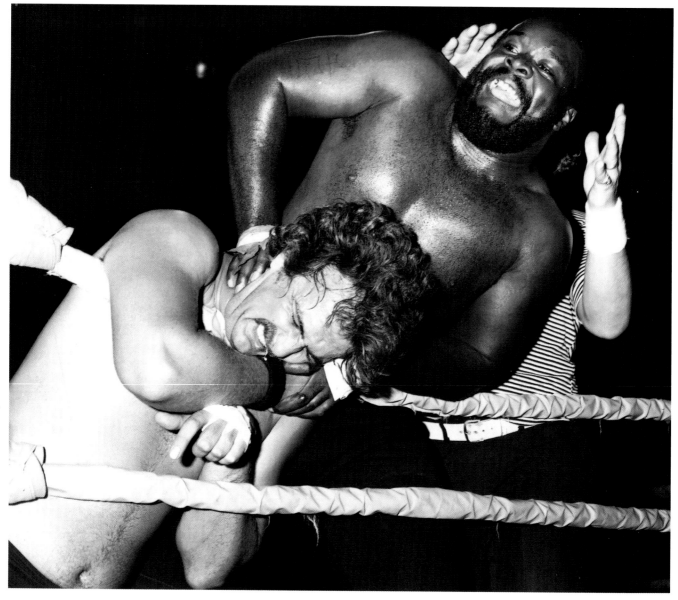

JAKE "THE SNAKE" ROBERTS CHOKED OUT ON THE ROPES (1978–1979),
FACING PAGE: RITTER PUTS PLENTY OF POWER INTO A FIST DROP ON JAKE
"THE SNAKE" ROBERTS (1978–1979)

and Ritter's co-worker got Sonny King to train him. He began his wrestling career in 1977.

After only a few matches, he went to Memphis, where somebody must have been impressed with his size. In August of 1978, Bruce Hart and Dynamite Kid were working in Bielfeld, Germany. Ritter had arrived about two weeks earlier and was such a poor wrestler that he was being fired in the middle of the tour, which was unheard of.

Again, timing was everything. The top heel in the Calgary territory, Kasavubu managed by John Foley had just left and the promotion was sold on the idea of having a white-womanizing big black stud as its top heel. Big Daddy Ritter, still terribly green but close to 300 pounds,

was immediately put on top because Stu Hart wanted someone to fill the Kasavubu spot, and he always had a fondness for big football players. Dog used to tell people that when he started wrestling in Calgary, the Harts never smartened him up to the business. The first few weeks he was out there fighting for real, knocking guys around with real tackles, before Foley, an old-time shooter, started calming him down and teaching him the ropes.

Ritter quickly became a reasonably good heel interview, although he showed no signs of impending superstardom. With the foursome of Ritter and a nearly as green version of Jake Roberts generally facing the likes of a green Bret Hart, along with Dynamite Kid, who was already a super worker, the Calgary territory did reasonably well in late 1978 and early 1979.

Big Daddy clamps a face claw on a young Jake "The Snake" Roberts (1978–1979), *facing page:* Ritter slams Jake Roberts to the mat with a Russian leg sweep (1978–1979)

Ritter had a five-month run as North American champion, with Roberts doing a babyface turn and capturing the title from him in April 1979. When NWA world champion Harley Race was brought in for the annual summer Stampede show, it marked the first time Ritter would challenge for the world heavyweight title. After regaining the title from Roberts in August, he got word that Jake's father would be involved in a new wrestling promotion that was opening up. Ritter dropped the belt to Larry Lane and he and Roberts arrived in Louisiana at about the same time Watts broke away from Leroy McGuirk and started up Mid South Wrestling, promoting in what was thought to be a dead wrestling area of Louisiana and Mississippi. Watts' first and, without question, his most successful creation, was the Junkyard Dog. ▶

When the decision was made to go all the way, the

angle was created to build not only a top wrestling star, but a folk hero for the masses. Watts decided to copy the most famous angle in Los Angeles wrestling history which led to the 1971 Fred Blassie vs. John Tolos match at the Coliseum. They would blind the Dog, teasing that his career was over, and then when he defied the doctors' odds and came back anyway, he'd be made. First, he was made into a main event player when he won both the Louisiana and Mississippi titles, and then he and Buck Robley defeated The Fabulous Freebirds to win the Mid South tag team titles. Then in an angle, Michael Hayes sprayed the infamous Freebird hair removing cream into the Dog's eyes, blinding him. By this time, Mid South Wrestling was starting to garner some very impressive local television ratings, the territory was already popping, and the Dog was becoming something of a well-known celebrity in those markets. Literally, to protect the territory, Dog wasn't allowed to leave his house for fear of anyone seeing that he really wasn't blind. While this was going on, fans in the territory began sending money. Some $600 to $800 per week came in, mainly in $5 bills, from fans, probably most of whom were poor themselves, who acted like a member of their own family had been blinded in an accident and was unable to pay his bills.

Then came the crushing blow. Dog's daughter, LaToya, known to his friends as Kisha, was born, and it was heavily pushed on television as they did interviews with the blinded Dog that he couldn't even see the birth of his first daughter due to Michael Hayes. They portrayed it as if there were no guarantee his sight would ever return. To set up the final angle for the big match, the blinded Dog was brought to the Downtown Municipal Auditorium to thank the fans, and perhaps say goodbye to them for the last time. Today this would be angle alert, but in those days people didn't see it coming. Naturally the Freebirds, a threesome of Hayes, Terry Gordy and Buddy Roberts, showed up and some sort of an angle was going to take place. Exactly what it was, only a few people know, because it didn't happen. Instead, a fan hopped the rail with a gun, and aimed it right at Hayes, screaming, "Don't worry Dog, I'm covering you." Dog, selling he was blind, didn't know what to do, but fortunately security hit

the ring en masse and the gunman was disarmed. He was no doubt taken to what was known as "the room," a place where the police would shut the door and give horrible beatings to out of control fans, hopefully dissuading them from ever becoming part of the act. It wasn't unusual, after the police were done, for them to let the wrestler, if the fan had punched him, or Watts, who was a huge and sometimes vicious person, into the room and to close the door behind them as well.

Still supposedly blinded, the Junkyard Dog demanded to come back for one last match, a dog collar match with Hayes, where he could feel him, and could drag him around. It goes without saying what the end result of that match was. Actual records of what this match drew are no longer around but there is no question it was the largest indoor wrestling crowd in history up to that point, and set attendance records locally that stand to this day. At the time it was reported as drawing in excess of 36,000 fans, but that figure was likely exaggerated and was probably just shy of 30,000. Over the next few days, they took the same angle on the road to other cities in the market, selling out and drawing a record house in every venue. For the week, Junkyard Dog earned $12,000, a figure that nobody in wrestling earned in those days. It may have been the first monster house that he drew, but it was far from the last. When the Dog miraculously regained his

▶ **Bill Watts is generally given credit for coming** up with Junkyard Dog's famous ring name, from a line out of the Jim Croce classic, "Bad Bad Leroy Brown." At the time, the Dog would come into the ring with a wheelbarrow full of junk. After thumping his foes, he'd put them in the wheelbarrow. In 1980, Watts made what was actually considered a revolutionary decision within pro wrestling to make him the unquestioned and unbeatable top babyface star of the promotion, a black Bruno Sammartino. Other promoters from around the country thought he was nuts, believing that white fans would never support a pro wrestling show where the top babyface of the company was black. The wheelbarrow was dumped, replaced with a dog collar, and added to the mix was his entrance music, "Another one Bites the Dust."

eyesight and he wrestled for a while wearing protective goggles, New Orleans would usually pack them in every Monday. When it came time to blow off the big angles at the Superdome four or five times a year, the crowds for the next few years were usually upwards of 20,000. Between 1980 and 1983 with Junkyard Dog on top, it is probable that no city in North America drew as many fans to pro wrestling as New Orleans.

After coming back from that angle, Watts fed the Dog one foe after another every week, carefully protecting him at all times. Just after the Freebird angle, Len Denton was brought in as the Masked Grappler, an arrogant heel whose gimmick was that he could wrestle, and in his first television match, took Junkyard Dog down and rode him to get his gimmick over, probably not realizing what the game was supposed to be. Watts was furious, and nearly fired Denton on the spot. It is belived to be the only televised match in the history of Mid South Wrestling that Watts couldn't put his spin on and let air. The big angles, usually a tag team partner turning on him, whether Paul Orndorff, Ted DiBiase, Buck Robley, Mr. Olympia (Jerry Stubbs) or finally Butch Reed, were saved until just before a Superdome date. Watts used to tap into reality using things he knew Junkyard Dog's audience knew about him to add heat. The Dog was actually best man at DiBiase's wedding and everybody in the know was familiar with that. Imagine the heat when DiBiase turned on the Dog.

"There were nights in New Orleans when I quit taking my car to the building because I was afraid it would be destroyed," DiBiase remembered. "I'd drive with Grizzly (Smith) and they'd slash his tires. Sometimes I had to leave the building hiding in the trunk of a car."

While all this was going on, he was, according to a local newspaper survey, the most popular athlete in New Orleans, particularly among the kids. At the time, the top football star was Archie Manning and the top basketball star was Pete Maravich, both white, and Junkyard Dog and Michael Spinks were the lone black sports heroes.

But if the rise of Junkyard Dog was meteoric, the fall was a lot slower and more painful. He was earning about $150,000 per year as Watts' top draw, for a life consisting largely of going to the gym, travelling, partying in all those towns as a celebrity, and wrestling. Buddy Landel, who

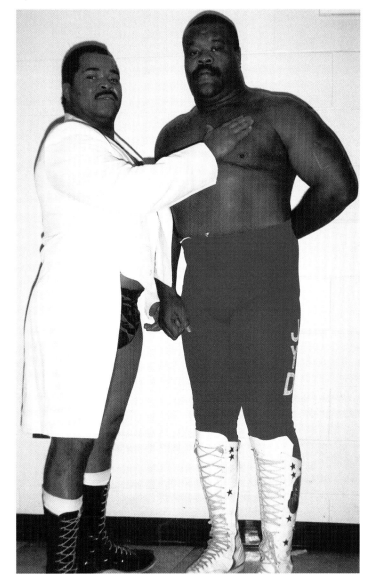

JUNKYARD DOG WITH HIS FORMER ROOMMATE AND TAG TEAM PARTNER, PISTOL PEZ WHATLEY, *FACING PAGE:* JUNKYARD DOG WITH JOHN FOLEY IN STAMPEDE WRESTLING

was his next-door neighbor, used to drive him from city to city and remembered Dog always giving money away to people down on their luck. As with many wrestlers in that circuit, the travel made his marriage fall apart, although in the case of Junkyard Dog, the fall was far more pronounced as his wife ended up having to be institutionalized. Whether it was those problems, or just the ready access from being a rich celebrity, the cocaine came at about the same time. He stopped training, and his once hard body ballooned to around 300 pounds again. While his ring work was never good, it actually got worse. Watts tried his best to camouflage the problem. He would explain Dog's weight gain as him having to bulk up to face the likes of Kimala and King Kong Bundy. Still,

business was strong, largely because Watts had replenished his ranks with some strong undercard performers who carried the wrestling end of the show. But the weekly Monday night shows at the Downtown Municipal Auditorium were badly damaged when Mr. Wrestling II scored a three count on Dog to win the North American title on March 12, 1984. Suddenly, people started to think that their hero had taken a dive on them, or perhaps maybe pro wrestling really was b.s. But the rest of the circuit remained strong, as did the big Superdome shows. Junkyard Dog was starting to fade, both physically and as a draw. His drug problems were getting worse and were causing him financial problems. At about the same time, the offer from the WWF came.

In those days it was traditional for a wrestler leaving a territory to give four weeks notice so he could be written out of the storylines. For a headliner, six weeks was considered more professional. However, without warning, Dog simply disappeared, leaving a string of no-shows in main events against Hacksaw Butch Reed in every market on the circuit, and he showed up immediately on WWF television. One night about a year or so after his arrival, probably at his peak as far as WWF drawing power, Junkyard Dog returned to the Superdome to form a tag team with Hulk Hogan, but only drew about 6,000 fans. The magic was over. At about that time, Dog's ex-wife either escaped or was released from the mental hospital, went to his parents' house and kidnapped back her daughter, who was living there while Dog was doing 28-straight-day runs for the WWF. He immediately chartered a plane home, went to her brother's house and broke down the door. The brother, who was a local police officer, tried to stop him, and the two scrambled trying to be the first to get a gun, which went off, shooting the police officer in the side of his stomach. It was ruled an accidental shooting.

Junkyard Dog's run at the top in the WWF would have lasted a lot longer, but his problems worsened. He started no-showing dates and eventually lost his job. He was nicknamed Junkfood Dog within the industry because of his fondness for twinkies, candy bars and midnight snacks, and over the years his weight increased to around 330 pounds. He got numerous second chances

A PLAIN AND SIMPLE CHOKE ON JIM "THE ANVIL" NEIDHART
(1978–1979)

because there were few people around with his name and charisma. He got married again, and when that marriage broke up, he lost his car, his jewelry, and his home.

Dog's last big run in the business came in 1990-91 with WCW. Ole Anderson was the booker and trying to get the black fans back in the Southeast with a Junkyard Dog vs. Ric Flair run. The matches were horrible and didn't draw all that well. Dog stuck around for a while in mid-cards before fading to the indie-world, where the reputation that ruined his career largely continued.

Over the last few years, Dog never had a stable home address. According to friends, he made several unsuccessful attempts to lick his problems. At one point he worked for Walmart in Las Vegas. He later bounced around to his old stomping grounds, trying to hustle indie dates based on his old name. He had tried to get back with WWF and WCW but neither company was willing to take the chance on a guy who had little going for him, other than the fact he was an incredible draw for a short period and was a recognized name as part of a national wrestling boom that was long over. He was living with a family in Mississippi and working in their repossession business.

On June 1, he drove back to his home town of Wadesboro, NC for LaToya's high school graduation, his daughter born during the Freebird angle. He arrived a few hours too late. The graduation was already over, and she had left with her friends to spend the night hanging out at the beach. The next morning, when she found out he had driven in to see her, it was combined with the news that he had just died in a car accident.

Wearing a t-shirt, Junkyard Dog was buried in Wadesboro, NC on June 6. The man who had earned and drawn a few million dollars in the ring had only one member of the wrestling community at his funeral, his former traveling mate Landel. WWF, WCW and several of his former foes like The Funks and DiBiase sent flowers. Another person who sent his best wishes to the funeral director was Michael Jordan. But it seemed that the entire town came out for the funeral, some 1,500 to 2,000 strong. They remembered him as the one of them who made it out, all the way to the top of the world, and for a brief period, created magic.

Shohei "Giant" Baba passed away at 4:04 PM on January 31, 1999, due to bowel cancer. Baba belongs with only Antonio Inoki and El Santo when it came to people everyone in their culture knew, a status Americans who think of Hulk Hogan in that category could never imagine. He was a national star for nearly four decades, and his longevity made him bigger than Rikidozan, the most famous of the sumos or even baseball legends like Sadaharu Oh and Shigeo Nagashima.

Some say that Baba was the wealthiest man ever in the wrestling industry, although he was very private regarding his personal finances. Those closest to him believe the only man in the industry wealthier is McMahon. Baba parlayed the millions he made promoting and wrestling into land and real estate investments in Hawaii and Japan starting in the early '60s, in addition to stock market investments that made him a multi-millionaire.

As a promoter, he was one of the greatest innovators in history, developing concepts that stood the test of time. He used the biggest name talent and some of the biggest egos in the business, but even when it went against the grain of his headliners' style in other promotions, they all knew that finishes were not negotiable.

He was the promoter everyone wanted to work for because of his reputation for honesty and because he paid more for top talent than any other promoter in the world, guaranteed. (In the '90s, by not adapting to the changes in the industry, that reputation changed.) His young boys grew up to be the best workers the business would produce in the modern era, starting out as teenagers washing his back, tying and untying his wrestling boots, running messages and carrying his bags so that when they got a top position, they realized how hard they had worked to earn it and they respected it. ▶

Baba promoted wrestling in a manner contrary to common wisdom, and up until the last two or three years of his life, was very successful. Common wisdom in promoting wrestling is to give the audience the product it wants to see, adapting constantly to keep up with changing tastes. Baba's philosophy was different. To him, his role as a promoter was to educate the public and his wrestlers to appreciate his vision of what good wrestling is, and to accept it. He was almost always successful doing so. But it's a lot harder to promote, because it requires a physically demanding style to make up for eliminating the gimmick-oriented shortcuts and angles. Without the easy gimmicks and all but the most basic of angles, it is harder for a wrestler to get over and greatly limits him. Baba's style could only be successful when presented with the top talent to be found in the world, and fortunately for Baba, more often than not, he had enough of it to make it work. Because of that, his style produced more legendary matches than any other. ▶

Baba was the first to book foreigners on the "Japanese" side in feuds, first Destroyer, and later the Funks, breaking the traditional Japanese vs. Geijin mentality when it came to the main events. He created the concept of the acrobatic masked man, aimed directly at the children's demographic with Mil Mascaras. New Japan took that to the next level years later with the first Tiger Mask. Baba recognized in 1988 that the second incarnation of the Universal Wrestling Federation (UWF) had become the hottest wrestling company in the world and his

> ▶ **"He wanted to be on that bus. He could have** lived his life in France on the Riviera," noted Terry Funk, who worked with him in the formation of All Japan Pro Wrestling (AJPW) and booked for the company for the next 15 years. "He loved doing it that much. He had no need for anything else."

GIANT SHOHEI BABA ENTERS THE RING IN HIS CLASSIC ROBE

business was starting to have to play catch-up. Baba totally overhauled his booking philosophy. He'd spent 16 years of having frequent and predictable double count out finishes in the big matches to protect egos and unbeatable reputations for the top stars, and by 1990 had gone to an all clean finish format, eliminating DQs (disqualifications) and CORs (counts out of the ring). It led to the hottest period of business in company history.

Shohei Baba was born on January 23, 1938 in Sanjyo, a small city near Niigata in Central Japan. He was the ace of the Sanjyo High pitching staff and known for having an overpowering fastball. He gained enough local notoriety that he was scouted by the Yomiuri (Tokyo) Giants, the national's Major League baseball powerhouse, and was signed at the age of 16 while still in his junior year of high school. His major league career was the proverbial cup of coffee, more notable because he was then the tallest man ever to play major league baseball in Japan. He played only three games late in the 1957 season, finishing with an 0-1 record, and was sent back down to the minors for more seasoning. The Giants dropped his contract after the 1959 season and he signed with the Taiyo Whales for 1960, but as legend has it, before the season started, he slipped and fell in the bathtub, destroyed the nerves in his arm and his baseball career was history.

Baba was sent to Mitsuhiro Momota Sr. (Rikidozan), by this time a national hero and owner of the Japanese Wrestling Association. Rikidozan was getting to the age where he realized to keep his business strong, he'd have to start grooming a successor to his throne. In April of 1960, Baba entered Rikidozan's dojo as one of his two hot prospects for future superstardom, the other being a

Brazilian high school track star of Japanese descent named Kanji Inoki. The two trained together under Rikidozan, and made their debuts on September 30, 1960 at the old Daito Ku Gymnasium in Tokyo where Baba beat Yonetaro Tanaka and Inoki, called Antonio Inoki to give him a more mysterious air, lost to Korean star Kintaro Oki. Over the next few months they wrestled on several occasions, always with Baba winning, before Baba was sent to the United States to gain experience and be brought back as a headliner a few years later.

Baba was the biggest Japanese star ever in the United States, almost from the moment he got off the plane in July 1961. Training under Fred Atkins, a surly old shooter from Toronto, and being booked around the country by The Great Togo, Baba was billed at 7'3" and more than 300 pounds (at the time he was probably about 260 pounds). He became an immediate freak attraction. Togo got him into every major territory as a headliner and he was one of the biggest draws during period of renewed wrestling interest. While big money was earned, Togo apparently got the lion's share. Baba himself recalled getting $25 a night while headlining the biggest arenas, and surviving on one meal a day. He never looked at his run as an American superstar as a happy time.

Under the name Baba the Giant, he became a big attraction in the Northeast, including many heel vs. heel main events in 1962 against NWA world champion Buddy Rogers. He generally worked as the heel either on top, or underneath Rogers against the top faces of the day such as Bruno Sammartino, Johnny Valentine, Bearcat Wright, Argentina Rocca and Edouard Carpentier. Sammartino's first ever loss at Madison Square Garden, on a count out, came on November 13, 1961 to Baba as the

GIANT BABA DEFENDS THE NWA WORLD TITLE AGAINST JACK
BRISCO (KIEL AUDITORIUM IN ST. LOUIS, 1974)

semifinal to a Rogers vs. Rocca match that drew 20,253 fans. His feud with The Destroyer over the WWA (World Wrestling Association) world title sold out the Olympic Auditorium in Los Angeles.

Togo sent Baba back to Japan in March 1963 for the annual World League tournament amidst great fanfare. He wrestled to a forty-five minute draw with Killer Kowalski in his first match back in Japan on March 24, 1963 at Sumo Hall, causing Rikidozan to remark to many that his successor had been found.

Probably the best example of Baba's American stardom came at the end of his U.S. run, in February 1964. During that month, he faced and put over Lou Thesz for the NWA world title in both Detroit and Cincinnati, Sammartino for the WWWF world title in Madison Square Garden before 14,764 fans, and finished the month challenging Blassie for the WWA world title at the Olympic. Few if any wrestlers in American history ever challenged for all three major world titles during the same month. By this point he was earning substantial money in the United States when the JWA (Japanese Wrestling Association), in danger of closing shop, wanted him back. Business being what it was, the JWA could make no promises he'd be able to earn what he'd been making in the United

States. Togo told him to stay, but he didn't listen, ending their business relationship and returning home.

He literally saved the business. After the death of Rikidozan on December 8, 1963, in a gangland style nightclub stabbing, investigations into the death of the national idol revealed a heavy mob influence in the pro wrestling business. The image of the sport darkened and most major arenas refused to allow the shows in. Baba is best remembered as the perennial international heavyweight champion, whose quiet charisma and reputation that stayed untarnished in wrestling over four decades, cleaned up the image of the profession, wearing the same belt Rikidozan made famous by beating Lou Thesz. Baba beat all the top foreign stars of the day such as Sammartino, Blassie, Fritz Von Erich, Thesz, Bobo Brazil, Gene Kiniski, Kowalski, Don Leo Jonathan, The Destroyer, Dick the Bruiser, The Crusher, Wilbur Snyder and many more, eventually bringing the business back. His baseball stadium International title vs. NWA world title challenge against Kiniski on August 14, 1967 at Osaka Stadium, which ended as a sixty-five-minute draw – the longest title match ever in Japanese wrestling history – drew in excess of 25,000 fans, and was the match that Baba always considered the greatest of his career.

The period from 1967–71 is best remembered for the Baba and Inoki tag team, and was one of the legendary

GIANT BABA DEFENDS THE NWA WORLD TITLE AGAINST JACK BRISCO (KIEL
AUDITORIUM IN ST. LOUIS, 1974)

periods for the Japanese wrestling industry, with nightly
sellouts and huge television ratings. As international tag
team champions, Baba and Inoki first captured the titles
on October 31, 1967 in Osaka from Bill Watts and Tarzan
Tyler. Over the years they beat such teams as Kiniski and
Johnny Valentine, Fritz and Waldo Von Erich, Crusher
and Bruiser, The Funks, Snyder and Hodge, and Sammartino and Ray Stevens.

NTV (Nippon Television Network), which broadcasts
All Japan to this day and has covered pro wrestling nearly
every week since the '50s, carried the show and had Baba
under a big guarantee as a network star. In 1969, a fledg-
ling network called NET (later re-named TV Asahi which
grew into one of Japan's four major networks) went to
the JWA and Inoki to acquire broadcast rights for its own
wrestling show. The result was two hours of prime time,
one on Friday and the other on Monday on two different
networks, usually with a Baba singles match on NTV and
an Inoki match on NET as the main events. If there was a
tag match with both of them, it would alternate. The
boom in front of the scenes led to chaos behind the
scenes. The owners, Junzo Hasegawa (Yoshinosato) and
Kokichi Endo, paid almost no attention to American
wrestling and were lagging when it came to promoting
new foreign stars or understanding the ability of the tal-

ent they needed to bring in. In addition, they had vices
and the company was running out of money. Baba and
Inoki both wanted to start their own company. When
word reached the office, Inoki was fired, but they pro-
tected Baba as the top star. Baba didn't last much longer,
and set the wheels in motion for his own big move.

Inoki had started New Japan several months earlier in
1972, but in October, Baba, having just left the JWA, and with
the help of Dory Funk Sr. and NTV backing for television
rights, ran his first tour of AJPW, All Japan Pro Wrestling.

Despite having access to the top Americans, All Japan
was not an immediate success. Baba went to work to solve
this problem by bringing Destroyer in as a full-time regular
on the face side. He signed a wrestler out of the 1972
Olympics named Tomomi Tsuruta, who was an incredible
worker almost from his start in 1973 after training under
Dory Jr. in Amarillo, and then signed judo legend Geesink to
work as his tag partner on the face side. With the two companies at war for the top spot, Baba and Inoki also had their
personal rivalry, trying to convince fans who the top Japanese
wrestler was. With the International title in the hands of Kintaro Oki in Korea, Baba created his own, called the Pacific
Wrestling Federation title, in early 1973. With Inoki's popularity on the rise, Baba, to again try and position himself as
the man, purchased the NWA title for himself for a one week
period in 1974 (he did so again in both 1979 and 1980, and
also purchased the AWA title for a few months for Tsuruta to
give him credibility as an internationally recognized world
champion, and later for Stan Hansen in the '80s).

McMahon Sr.'s top star and world champion, Sammartino, out of loyalty and friendship to Baba, refused to
work for Inoki's New Japan which led to bitter disagree-
ments with McMahon, and it wasn't until Bob Backlund
got the WWWF title that McMahon was able to send his
world champion to work for New Japan.

In 1973, Sammartino, seeing the huge Baba squirming
to get out of his small car, gave Baba one of his old Cadillacs
as a gift. It cost Sammartino $3,000 to ship it to Japan, and
Baba repaid him on the next tour. Sammartino remarked to
the Japanese press that if Baba's business had ever hit rock
bottom, he'd have gone to Japan and worked for him for
free to help rebuild it, noting that he was the only promoter
he ever dealt with that he would say that about.

Eventually, New Japan got NWA membership. Baba

was able to keep New Japan from getting dates on the NWA world champion based on previous loyalty from that era's champion, Harley Race, against whom Baba had his best matches in the '70s. One of the reasons Dusty Rhodes, at the time the NWA's biggest drawing card, never had a lengthy run as champion – aside from some of the traditional old-line promoters not wanting him as their representative – was because Rhodes had booking ties with Inoki and the pro-Baba political forces kept him from a lengthy reign. By the time the early Ric Flair as NWA champion era came around, the political structure had changed and NWA membership was no longer considered important to New Japan. The two companies worked together briefly in 1979, running a joint show which sold out Budokan Hall. Inoki and Baba teamed together for the first time in eight years, beating Butcher and Tiger Jeet Singh. After the show, relations fell apart and the companies resumed the war.

New Japan started the most bitter part of the battle when it lured away Baba's long-time top heel, Butcher, with a promise of raising his salary from $4,000 to $8,000 per week, unheard of money for a wrestler in

those days. All Japan then did the same, and Baba promised Stan Hansen – New Japan's top foreign star and Inoki's biggest money rival – a lifetime deal. The Hansen deal, finalized months earlier at a secret meeting in Hawaii between Hansen, The Funks and Baba, was the biggest and most important jump of them all. Hansen had just finished his New Japan tour, teaming with Hogan in the tag team tournament. With the brief exception of a period when Brody's popularity peaked, Hansen held the status as the most popular foreign star ever to work Japan, one he retained until the last year or two of the '90s.

All Japan left New Japan near dead as they raided most of Inoki's disgruntled crew in 1984, led by his hottest star, Riki Choshu. All Japan ruled the roost for a few years and came close to ending the war for good, but then Choshu and most of his crew jumped back. Baba, one of the last powerful members of the NWA, continued to feature the champion prominently and cooperated with most of the top NWA promoters. But he was becoming more and more an island unto himself as the NWA began disintegrating in the face of the WWF's onslaught. His relations with Jim Crockett Jr., who was running the NWA, were strained when Crockett cancelled several advertised

Ric Flair tours, which resulted in breaking the long All Japan/NWA world title legacy. Baba was forced to make a deal to bring back Brody, who had been out of Japan for nearly a year after walking out on New Japan prior to a tag team tournament. The final straw for the long history of the NWA championship in All Japan came after Ted Turner bought JCP (Jim Crockett Promotions). A deal was made, for both the NWA and All Japan, to recognize a world six man tag championship team of Tenryu and The Road Warriors. The Road Warriors had become hot attractions for Baba and Crockett, and Tenryu was Baba's leading star. A title defense was scheduled as the main event of a Clash of the Champions on February 15, 1989 in Cleveland where they would defend against Junkyard Dog, Dick Murdoch and Michael Hayes. The NWA, soon to be known as WCW, set up an angle where Kevin Sullivan and his crew would lock a door, keeping the challengers from getting to the ring, and his crew would take over the match. To fans of traditional wrestling in Japan, this went way beyond a situation Baba could explain. He left the NWA, and WCW made a deal with New Japan after Baba opened up doing business with WWF.

WWF and All Japan ran a huge show at the Tokyo Dome on April 13, 1990, which also featured New Japan in a supporting role, but that relationship was doomed because of the gigantic ego clash between Baba and McMahon. Baba was insulted because he was advertising a Hulk Hogan title match on top, while WWF switched its title to Ultimate Warrior before the show and failed to let Baba know about it ahead of time.

During that same time period, Tenryu, Hara, Great Kabuki and several others jumped to billionaire Hachiro Tanaka's old and quickly doomed SWS (Super World Sports) promotion. This forced Baba, notoriously conservative about elevating top talent to fill spots, to start pushing wrestlers like Toshiaki Kawada, Kenta Kobashi, Akira Taue and Tsuyoshi Kikuchi into main events, which led the company to its best box office period in its history. The biggest move was taking the mask off Tiger Mask, and giving Mitsuharu Misawa the push as the new singles star by pinning Jumbo Tsuruta in one of the most emotional matches in company history on June 8, 1990 at Budokan

Hall. That show came close to a sellout, and Misawa caught fire because of his win against Jumbo.

Budokan Hall became the hotbed of pro wrestling, validating in Baba's mind his style of clean finishes. A string of sellouts in the building lasted for several years with the Triple Crown as the focal point. All Japan sold out more than 250 consecutive shows in Tokyo through the early to mid '90s, routinely drawing houses in the $1 million range eight times per year at Budokan Hall. At the company's peak, they would put tickets for the next Budokan show on sale at the live event, and completely sell out the next show.

For several years, during a down period for business world wide, Baba was drawing the biggest houses, producing the best television and providing the best wrestling matches anywhere in the world. Even though it peaked years earlier, Baba finally agreed to do a Dome show on May 1, 1998 and it was the most successful show he would ever promote, drawing 58,300 fans.

Eight days before his death, Baba was brought a tape of the Misawa vs. Kawada Triple Crown title change match. It is said it put a big smile on his face. It turned out to be the final wrestling match he would ever see. Baba had been diagnosed with colon cancer and underwent a first operation that was kept quiet. His failure to take his usual December vacation and canceling a trip to Vancouver, Canada for a WWF PPV show were explained by saying he was suffering from a bad cold. He had been released from hospital in late December with a positive prognosis. At the end of the first week of January, during a routine checkup, the cancer was found to have recurred and he was rushed immediately for a second operation which was made public but still kept relatively quiet. Culturally cancer is not spoken about in Japan. Even for his 61st birthday, no press or wrestlers were allowed to see him. Only his two closest friends, his wife, the ring announcer and the head referee were allowed to visit. Eight days later he was dead. He died as the last promoter still pushing the old style of wrestling, with lengthy main events, clean winners, and finishing moves that worked against the top stars. His passing marked the end of a chapter in the Japanese wrestling world.

SHOHEI "GIANT" BABA TOWERING OVER THE RING

Buddy Rogers

One of pro wrestling's all-time biggest drawing cards and arguably the greatest drawing heel in history, "Nature Boy" Buddy Rogers, passed away July 6, 1992 at the age of 71 in a Fort Lauderdale, FL hospital.

Rogers, who appeared to be the picture of health to the end, had suffered three strokes over two weeks prior to his death. The first was a mild one. The second and third, both on Monday, June 22, left him blind and paralyzed on one side of the body. He lapsed into a coma and was on life support systems by Wednesday of that week and officially passed away that Friday night.

Rogers, born Herman Rohde in Camden, NJ, although he later legally changed his name to Nature Boy Buddy Rogers, innovated and popularized many of the most enduring elements of today's pro wrestling. While not the first bleached blond villain (Gorgeous George popularized that look a few years earlier on national television), he was the first arrogant strutting blond with serious heel heat. ▶

Rogers was generally considered, and grudgingly so by many since he was not a popular performer in his prime, the best worker of the '50s. Many of Ric Flair's mannerisms in the ring – from the hair, the attitude, the robes, the tan, the begging off while in trouble down to the Nature Boy moniker and the figure four – were modern adaptations of concepts Rogers popularized.

During his prime Rogers was one of the most hated men in the business, not only by fans, but also by promoters. He was considered tough to do business with since he was more than well aware of his power at the box office. His fellow wrestlers had similar feelings, since he had a reputation for being a bully in the ring. As the years passed, though, he completely changed his image and became one of the nicest and most respected of the old-timers. He was also held in esteem for maintaining his remarkable physical condition. In the later years of his life, Rogers, whose career as a headliner was cut short by a 1963 heart attack, had attracted national publicity for his remarkable physique for a man pushing 70 in an Esquire Magazine article, then for punching out a bigger 29-year-old during a brawl in a sandwich shop. In January of 1992 he attempted to become the second man to wrestle professionally in seven decades (Lou Thesz being the first) by agreeing to a match with Buddy Landel on a card promoted by Joel Goodhart in Philadelphia. The match never took place, as Goodhart's promotion folded just days before. It was said to have had a strong advance and may have been a resounding success.

Rogers started wrestling in 1939 as Dutch Rohde while working as a police officer in New Jersey. He took the name of Nature Boy Buddy Rogers early in his career in Texas. Buddy Rogers was a futuristic character popular in '40s science fiction, while Nature Boy was a hit song during that same time. Rogers was one of the biggest names in the business during the first television boom in

▶ **Buddy Rogers was the first hardcore heel NWA** world champion. He popularized the figure four leglock (then called the figure four grapevine) and many aspects of working a match that are still being used today. He is generally considered the most enduring box office draw throughout North America from the period of 1948–63. Some, like Gorgeous George, were bigger draws for a short period of time, while others, like Argentina Rocca, were bigger draws on a more regional basis. His working style in the ring is considered the forerunner to two of the other greatest workers in the world during their time: Ray Stevens in the '60s and Ric Flair during the '80s.

of the late '40s when pro wrestling was being televised by the Chicago-based Dumont Network. In later years, when the business was struggling after being ravaged by television overexposure, Rogers, working out of Columbus, OH as the booker for promoter Al Haft, was the top drawing card nationally. Working in the Midwest as United States champion, Rogers was part of the revitalization of wrestling's popularity in that part of the country, particularly in Chicago where his main event matches sold out the International Amphitheater's 11,000 seats every other Friday night. After running through all the competition, Rogers faced the ultimate babyface, then-National Wrestling Alliance world heavyweight champion Pat O'Connor. The match is still, to this day, the biggest drawing NWA world title match in history and was attended by one of the largest paid crowds to see pro wrestling ever in the United States. Held on June 30, 1961 at Comiskey Park in Chicago, it drew 38,622 fans, a record that stood until 1987, and a $148,000 house, an American record which lasted nearly two decades. Rogers won two of three falls to become world champion in one of the most famous matches in pro wrestling history. A rematch between the two several months later at Comiskey Park, where Rogers retained the title, drew about 30,000 fans.

Lou Thesz credited Rogers for the success of two of the most famous promoters of the era, Eddie Quinn in Montreal and Sam Muchnick in St. Louis. Muchnick, after World War II, ran opposition to Martin Thesz (Lou's father) in St. Louis. The Thesz promotion was regularly drawing 10,000 per show while Muchnick's shows were struggling to draw 2,000 to 4,000. When Muchnick brought Rogers in, it resulted in his first sellout ever in 1949 against Don Eagle. It wasn't long before the two groups merged with Muchnick running the promotion and Lou Thesz as NWA champion. "He was barely surviving," Thesz remembered, "But when Al Haft gave him Buddy, he turned it around." ▶

Rogers became more and more difficult to book by promoters outside the Northeast. On August 31, 1962, Rogers was in a dressing room in Columbus, OH when Karl Gotch and Bill Miller, two of the legendary tough guys of the business, caught Rogers and smashed his hand. The injury caused him to miss several big money title defenses. The incident apparently occurred when Gotch challenged Rogers, who doubled as the booker for Al Haft's crew, to a fight. Rogers headed for the door and as he tried to get out, Miller slammed it on him. Not long after he returned, on November 21, 1962 in Montreal, Rogers had a title defense against Killer Kowalski, which wound up with Rogers getting his ankle broken in the first minute of the match. He was pinned for the first fall, and obviously did not wrestle a second. After much controversy, since Kowalski wasn't supposed to win the title, the NWA tried to save face by making a ruling that, since it was a two out of three fall match and Kowalski only won one fall, Rogers was still recognized as champion. Finally the NWA/WWWF split occurred when Rogers returned to action. Thesz, then in semi-retirement, was brought back by the NWA to win the title from Rogers and Rogers missed their first two meetings due to the hand injury.

Thesz' dislike for Rogers was well-known. Thesz would never do a job for Rogers, once remarking, "there

▶ **While Rogers as champion meant big box office, it was probably the most controversial** championship reign in the history of the NWA and eventually was responsible for the formation of the WWWF, today's WWF. Wrestling lore has it that Toots Mondt attempted to gain a stranglehold on the business. Mondt, a legendary shooter/promoter, was part of the famous "trust" threesome with Strangler Lewis and Billy Shadow that was the first group to control pro wrestling nationally during the '20s. Mondt was at the time promoting in the Northeast as a partner with, among others, Vince McMahon, Sr. The most prestigious power in the sport was gaining control of the NWA championship, held by Rogers, who was his man. Mondt is generally given credit for this series of events. Ultimately McMahon later aced out Mondt for full control of the Northeastern cities and was the ultimate beneficiary in the formation of the WWWF.

ROGERS IN HIS LATER CAREER (LIKELY LATE '60S; TROPHY AND TITLE BELT UNKNOWN)

Legends reunited – Fabulous Moolah, Lou Thesz and Buddy Rogers (l to r)

isn't enough whiskey in Canada to get me to put Rogers over." Just before the Toronto match scheduled for January 24, 1963, Muchnick, who was the leading power behind the NWA, posted a $25,000 bond to insure them either doing the job when the time came or not running off with the title. He told Rogers that if he no-showed the match, then Muchnick was going to release his bond and give it all to charity. Rogers did the job for Thesz, but legend has it the match was made one fall specifically so that if Rogers wasn't cooperative, Thesz could take him out.

When he lost the NWA title, the Northeastern promoters who were against Rogers dropping pulled out of the NWA and formed the WWWF, with Rogers as the first champion. With the exception of Flair, Rogers is the only man to hold both the NWA and the WWWF (now WWF) titles. Rogers suffered a heart attack shortly thereafter, but as soon as he could return, came back for a series of two-minute matches and was carried by partners like Buddy Austin and Johnny Barend in tag matches. This led up to his dropping the title to Bruno Sammartino on May 17, 1963 in Madison Square Garden in 47 seconds. This began Sammartino's near-seven-year run as WWWF champion. Rogers did some wrestling, mainly around Montreal, after recovering, but for the most part was retired by 1964. He made a brief comeback a few years later for The Sheik in Detroit, then disappeared from the scene once again.

In 1978, he made a surprise return, wrestling as a main event babyface in Florida for about one year. He then left for the Carolinas, as a heel manager of Jimmy Snuka, Ken Patera and a few others. He also wrestled three matches against a babyface Flair that are now legendary. Sometime later, Rogers wound up in the WWWF doing "Rogers' Corner," an interview segment that was the forerunner of "Piper's Pit," as a babyface. He wound up as manager of Snuka in 1982 when Snuka made his babyface turn on Lou Albano. Rogers wrestled a few tag matches with Snuka against Albano and Stevens before suffering a broken hip prior to a scheduled match in Madison Square Garden, at which point his association with the WWF ended over a lawsuit and he retired. In

"NATURE BOY" ROGERS

1984, Rogers and Larry Sharpe opened up the original Monster Factory, but Rogers later moved from his long-time New Jersey home and retired to Lauderdale-by-the-Sea, FL.

Rogers, who underwent quadruple heart bypass surgery several years before his death, was known for keeping up a daily training regimen of swimming and doing weight lifting to preserve the physique that made him famous. About one month before he died, he slipped in a supermarket and broke his arm in three places. He dropped about 20 pounds while in rehabilitation, and suffered a mild stroke which left his speech slurred. Later he collapsed from a second major stroke while taking a shower. His wife called 911 and he was taken to the hospital. While in a conversation at the hospital that day, he had the third stroke, which left him blind and paralyzed and he lapsed into a coma which he never came out of.

John William Minton, under the ring name Big John Studd, was one of pro wrestling's biggest draws and most famous personalities during the period the World Wrestling Federation went national. At 6'7" and 320 pounds during the mid-'80s, John Studd was one of the biggest wrestlers in the world at the time, and was a frequent opponent for André the Giant and Hulk Hogan in the WWF. The matches were hardly classics, but they were a strong part of a package that paved the way for the early Wrestlemanias that pioneered national broadcasts of pro wrestling.

He discovered he'd contracted Hodgkins Disease in November 1993, shortly after being a last minute fill-in for a match in October for his trainer, Walter "Killer" Kowalski in New England against Honkytonk Man. Studd had his wife courier his wrestling gear to town to be a fill-in. While he was limited as a performer to begin with, he got in the ring that night and realized he had no stamina whatsoever. He and everyone watching knew something was wrong. Shortly thereafter, he was taking a shower and washing under his arms and felt a hard lump. He was also having chest pains. He went to the doctor who took X-rays and found a large tumor in the middle of his chest. He tried to keep the news quiet, and when it broke, he downplayed the severity of his condition – except to his closest friends – until the end.

Studd had been in Fairfax Hospital near his home in Burke, VA for the ten days leading to his death. During 1994, he spent approximately 20 weeks in hospital fighting Hodgkins Disease which went into remission first after chemotherapy, came back, and went into remission again after a bone marrow transplant. His lungs collapsed six weeks before his death, but he recovered from

JOHN STUDD VS. PAUL ORNDORFF

that as well. He started running a fever, was suffering terrible joint pain, all symptoms of the cancer recurring. He passed away on March 20, 1995 from liver cancer after a 17-month battle with Hodgkins Disease. He had three children: 14-year old John Jr., 11-year old Janelle and four-year old Sean.

Minton wrestled for 18 years after playing college basketball. Originally from Butler, PA, after college he gravitated toward Los Angeles and was training there under Charlie Moto in early 1972 when Kowalski was in town as the top heel. Kowalski helped break Minton in and Minton always credited Kowalski as his trainer and remained loyal to him. He started in California as The Mighty Minton, a large prelim wrestler. He returned home and worked in a glorified jobber role for the old WWWF under the ring name Chuck O'Connor.

"We met in Los Angeles and were tag teaming together, usually against the Tolos Brothers," remembered Billy Graham. "We would potato those guys to death. We used to joke about how the poor Tolos Brothers had to deal with our inexperience. Studd and I were both so green and so big and strong at the time that we practically beat them to death. John (Tolos) would get in the ring with Studd and tell him to tag me. Then I'd get in with Chris (Tolos) and he'd tell me to tag Studd."

His second WWWF stint was in 1976 with Kowalski as The Masked Executioners holding the tag team titles, which was his first major career push. Because of his size, unique in wrestling at the time, he was a headliner for most of the remainder of his career.

It was in Texas in 1977 that he picked up the name Big John Studd, which probably helped a great deal as far as his name recognition when wrestling went national seven years later. He had first come in under the name Captain USA, under a mask and ring costume similar to WCW's Patriot, as

a heel feuding with the likes of Fritz Von Erich, Bruiser Brody and Stan Hansen. When he was unmasked, it was Houston promoter Paul Boesch who came up with the name he used most of the rest of his career.

After working based out of Hawaii for about a year, he was part of the package when Jim Crockett Jr.'s Mid Atlantic territory went on fire using young wrestlers who were to become superstars in the business like Ric Flair, Ricky Steamboat and Greg Valentine. Studd worked against one of the few wrestlers of that period who rivalled him for size in Blackjack Mulligan (Bob Windham). Studd used to tell his kids that when they looked around the house, they should always thank Mulligan and André because they were the ones who made most of it possible. ▶

Studd was billed at between 6'6" and 6'8" during the bulk of his career. When the WWF went national, his billed height moved toward the 6'10" or even 6'11" mark to give him even more of a monster appeal. He claimed to be "the real Giant" of pro wrestling for his feud with André. He took to wearing thick lifts in his wrestling boots to accentuate his height as a gimmick and to give him the visual appearance of being the same height as André.

Studd did well with his money, investing his wrestling earnings into local real estate around Virginia and Maryland. He was able to retire from wrestling and be financially well off enough that he never had to look back. He had largely gotten wrestling out of his blood before becoming friends with the 7'2" Ron Reis, a college basketball star out of Santa Clara University who grew up being a fan of Studd's during his WWF heyday. Reis always talked of possibly getting into wrestling. Studd introduced him to Kowalski and wanted to manage and team with Reis as a tag team called The Giants when he got his first major break with either the WWF or WCW.

Larry Matysik, who worked in the St. Louis office in the late '70s, recalled it was Studd's reputation as a basketball player as opposed to a wrestler that first got him into St. Louis, then considered the wrestling capital of North America. Sam Muchnick had agreed to coach a team of wrestlers against the local media in a celebrity

basketball game in early 1978 and was trying to load up the wrestlers' side with guys who could actually play basketball. They brought in Studd, who had never worked in St. Louis, as a ringer of sorts.

After leaving the Carolinas and having a short stint in Georgia, Studd wound up with a lengthy tenure in the AWA forming a tag team with Jerry Blackwell and feuding with the likes of Mad Dog Vachon and The Crusher in the early '80s.

"He wasn't happy in the AWA," said Matysik, who used him in St. Louis, generally in the semifinals to put over babyfaces they were pushing for upcoming title matches. "He never got the push there he thought he deserved."

After leaving the AWA in 1981, he started the first of his three singles tours as a star with the WWF. The first run was as a foe for both André and Bob Backlund at all the big arenas throughout the northeast. After a brief run in Florida feuding on top with Dusty Rhodes, he returned to the northeast, this time as Vince McMahon Jr. positioned himself for the national expansion. While never the focal player on the heel side, Studd, the first WWF protege of Bobby Heenan, was a key element doing the monster bit underneath, or working on top against Hogan or André. Perhaps his most famous angle was when he and Ken Patera cut André's hair off. Later he and King Kong Bundy formed a tag team for another run for André, and later the abortive feud with André and Bill Eadie as The Masked Machines. Well off financially and wanting to make it in Hollywood (he had a bit part in a Dudley Moore comedy with a few other wrestlers while in the WWF), he left pro wrestling in 1987 and did some

---

▶ **At no time was Studd ever a classic worker or even an average worker.** He was a very big man during a period in wrestling when there were only about three or four others with that kind of size. The biggest draw of them all was André. Studd, along with Ernie Ladd and Mulligan, was one of the only men who came within a few inches of the 6'10" André and drew huge money programmed against him.

KERRY VON ERICH WALLOPS A MASKED BIG JONH STUDD (DALLAS, 1978)

BIG JON STUDD VS. JOHN WELLS

acting gigs. While filming the movie "Marlboro Man," he was doing a stunt where he fell off his motorcycle. He would later tell some that he believed the jarring to his system from the fall caused the Hodgkins Disease.

While most wrestlers knew Studd used steroids, he hid it from his closest non-wrestler friends and always vehemently denied it to outsiders and the media. Those in wrestling remarked that Studd saw the kind of money André made and always wanted to reach that sort of freakish size. That may have led him to being a pioneer among wrestlers in the use of human growth hormone.

"A wrestling magazine did a story showing before and after pictures of 10 or 15 wrestlers including John," said Billy Graham. "The width between his eyes had widened by an inch at least because of the growth hormone. It enlarged the bones in his forehead. At the time he thought the growth hormone was safer than steroids."

Studd admitted to Graham that one of his doctors said it was a possibility that the growth hormone could have accelerated the onset of the Hodgkins Disease. While Studd never had a bodybuilder look, his weight probably approached 400 pounds later in his career. His limited mobility was made worse by the added weight, particularly the stress on his knees which plagued him greatly during his WWF comeback.

Studd had his final WWF run in 1989, this time as a babyface to feud with André, who had turned heel. McMahon gave Studd a major push. However Studd had gained about 40 pounds since his previous stint which had greatly slowed him down. Added to that were André's own health problems and the fact that André had gotten a lot moodier as his physical condition had deteriorated. One night André actually fell asleep in the ring with Studd and Studd had to hold a headlock on him while trying to wake him up. Studd was unhappy earning only $3,500 per week in a top spot. He had earned much more in his previous stint on top, although the André-Studd feud was a disappointment at the box office. He was unhappy with his Wrestlemania payoff and walked out of the WWF in the middle of the run. He wrestled a few matches as favors for Kowalski after that but, for the most part, never returned to wrestling. ▶

WALKING AMONG THE FANS, STUDD WAS A SIGHT TO BEHOLD

▶ **In the McMahon trial during the summer of 1994, John Studd was forced to admit, under oath,** in a strange scene via telephone from his home, that he had used steroids. The government called him as a witness despite protests from both McMahon and his lawyers. Studd claimed George Zahorian told him about a conversation he and McMahon had, where Zahorian told McMahon he was distributing steroids to his wrestlers and McMahon did not tell him to stop. It was the first public admission of what Studd had been trying to hide from all but his closest friends for the previous eight months. Suffering from Hodgkins Disease and weakened from the chemotherapy, he couldn't travel to New York for the trial.

Titan lawyers insisted that the illness not be mentioned. They were afraid the jury would tie his illness to the fact he admitted to purchasing steroids from Zahorian and used them regularly. Studd said at the trial that he believed Zahorian was doing himself and wrestlers in general a great service, because steroids were an important part of the wrestlers' regimen to help maintain their performance level.

Carl Raymond Stevens passed away in his sleep on the morning of May 3, 1995 at the age of 60 at his home in Fremont, CA. He was born September 5, 1935 in Point Pleasant, WV. He was Northern California's most famous wrestler. He produced its most famous angles and its most famous matches. Cause of death was believed to have been a heart attack, possibly from a bad reaction to booze and pills. He had been out drinking brandy and beer that night and took some pills before going to bed.

In the '60s, the general consensus within pro wrestling was that Ray Stevens had followed in the footsteps of Buddy Rogers as being the best all-around performer in the business. He combined great matches with the ability to make an opponent look great, but also was consistently one of the biggest money draws. He took big bumps and bounced his way around the ring, whether his opponent could work a lick or not, and continued doing it well into his 40s.

He was part of two of pro wrestling's all-time legendary tag teams with Nick Bockwinkel and Pat Patterson. His career started early, turning pro young, at the age of 15 after being a YMCA wrestler out of Columbus, OH. He burned the candle at both ends and in the middle for most of the next 45 years. Not only did he gain a reputation within the business as a world champion drinker and carouser but he also had a reputation as the greatest bump taker in a business of bump takers. He was fearless in many other sports and activities among a group of people that constantly tried to one-up each other. ▶

Roy Shire, who opened up a territory in Northern California in 1960, brought in his former tag team partner from Ohio, Indiana and Georgia, where the two, as the Shire Brothers, Roy and Ray, had held versions of the world tag team titles and made national headlines with a worked feud against famous boxer Archie Moore. On Shire's second show at the Cow Palace, Stevens defended his United States Champion title against Bill Melby. Stevens came into town and immediately began running down the city of San Francisco, talking about what a horrible place it was to live. He called foes, fans and television announcer Walt Harris pencil-neck geeks. People in San Francisco, one of the biggest tourist centers in the world, had never heard anyone insult their city before and had never had a promotion use television as strongly. The result was a sellout crowd for the debut of Stevens and the United States heavyweight title. When that was combined with Stevens' ability to work the crowd in the ring, it started a run of big houses with him on top that lasted the next 11 years right into the '70s.

In the early '50s, Pepper Gomez, a former bodybuilding champ who turned wrestler, became a big draw. He was being pushed in the area as the top babyface with a gimmick of being the man with the cast iron stomach. One night, as an angle, he let a succession of wrestlers jump onto his stomach off a stepladder.

Enter Ray Stevens, the heel who in the early '60s was the big star of a promotion that was already on fire. In a famous angle, Stevens came out and started yelling that the other wrestlers weren't jumping hard enough onto Gomez' stomach. So Gomez let him jump off the ladder, again to no effect. He then claimed the other wrestlers weren't

> ▶ **Stevens was a legend not just to the fans in** the area, but among the wrestlers themselves, for living a lifetime of wild antics. He coined the phrase that "God takes care of those who don't take care of themselves: little children, small animals and Ray Stevens."

POSSIBLY THE BEST WORKER OF THE '60S, RAY STEVENS

jumping from high enough, since all the jumps were from halfway up the ladder. So being the leading daredevil of his time, he climbed to the top of the ladder and jumped onto Gomez' stomach, who again didn't sell it. So Stevens did it one more time, and instead dropped his knee to Gomez' throat, called in those days the "Bombs Away." It became the most dreaded finishing maneuver in that part of the country. Gomez was coughing up blood by the end of the angle, and left the territory for several weeks.

When Gomez returned for his grudge match, it broke a record set by Elvis Presley for the largest crowd ever to attend an event at the Cow Palace in San Francisco – in excess of 17,000 fans – roughly 2,000 more than the building's capacity, with thousands more turned away. It earned $65,000 which stood as a Northern California record for nearly 20 years. The crowd is still the largest to ever watch pro wrestling in San Francisco. When it was over, with so many turned away, Shire started talking about sending the rematch to Candlestick Park and talked of breaking the Buddy Rogers-Pat O'Connor record for the biggest crowd in pro wrestling history set the year before.

It didn't materialize, as Stevens, who was as much if not more of a daredevil outside the ring as he was in it, broke his ankle in a go-cart race and was out of action for eight months. When he returned, Gomez had been programmed in another direction, and by the time the two could be brought back together, the fire wasn't there to do a ballpark show. However, largely based on that angle, Stevens and Gomez were able to draw against each other for the next five years in both singles and tag team matches before briefly forming a championship tag team.

"We had a lot of great matches," Gomez remembered. "Of all the wrestlers I ever faced, and I wrestled Lou Thesz, Verne Gagne, Killer Kowalski, Don Leo Jonathan, The Bruiser, (Edouard) Carpentier, Wilbur Snyder, Pat O'Connor, to me, he was the best heel I ever wrestled. I didn't like him at the time, but today I look back and smile a lot about it."

"I met him in 1965 in Australia for Jim Barnett," said

RAY STEVENS MAIN-EVENTING FOR THE U.S. TITLE VS. ED CARPENTIER IN SAN FRANCISCO

Dory Funk, who was later business partners with him in the '70s in the Amarillo promotion when Stevens and Terry Funk combined their wrestling with rodeo bulldogging. "Ray had been there for about a week before I got there and he was already the top draw. Ray and Mark Lewin had a great run in Australia. I worked with him in Melbourne and he did a fabulous job. An action shot of our match was in the newspaper. I saved it for a long time and wish I still had it. I think it may have been the only singles match we ever worked together."

While the Gomez angle and subsequent match was clearly the most famous, his matches with the likes of Cowboy Bob Ellis, Dick the Bruiser, Wilbur Snyder, Bobo Brazil, Domenic DeNucci, Big Bill Miller, Bearcat Wright, Bill Watts and Fritz Von Erich were also long remembered. On an international level, his most famous match during his reign as King of San Francisco was against Bruno Sammartino. Stevens was billed as world heavyweight champion on the West Coast while Sammartino was WWWF world champion and the king of the wrestling magazines, which were the only source of information outside the local region for the serious fans. Stevens scored a count out win in the July 15, 1967 match after using his "Bombs Away" in a title vs. title match at the Cow Palace. At that time, NWA rules allowed titles to change via count out which was considered a clean finish in the territory, although not on the East Coast. This technically enabled Sammartino to keep his title in his area while Stevens could be regarded as having cleanly beaten him in his. Stevens was announced as unified world champion that night, which fully established him in all the area fans' eyes as the top wrestler in the world.

With the exception of Gomez, his greatest area rival was probably his long-time tag team partner, Pat Patterson. Known as "The Blond Bombers" in their heyday, (Stevens' first nickname in California was Ray "Blond Bomber" Stevens), the two were considered by many to be the best tag team in the world in the '60s. They were the prototype of numerous teams that followed, including the Ric Flair and Greg Valentine tag team of the late '70s and even the Brian Pillman and Steve Austin tandem in WCW in 1993. By the time of their feud, the inevitable babyface turn had taken place, making Stevens the most popular wrestler ever to appear in the area until

SAN FRANCISCO'S TWO TOP BABYFACE HEROES, RAY STEVENS AND PAT
PATTERSON, *BOTTOM:* RAY STEVENS AND PAT PATTERSON — WORLD TAG TEAM
CHAMPIONS. PHOTO TAKEN AT THE CAULIFLOWER ALLEY CLUB ANNUAL
REUNION, SEVERAL MONTHS BEFORE RAY DIED, *FACING PAGE:* STEVENS ATOP
DR. BILL MILLER IN A BLOODY BRAWL IN SAN FRANCISCO'S FABLED COW
PALACE (1969)

the marketing of Hulk Hogan took wrestling by storm.
Even at his peak, Hogan never matched Stevens as a
draw in the area.

Ironically, the feud with Patterson had a similarity to
the Gomez feud. The two were set to have a grudge
match on August 9, 1969 at the Cow Palace for Stevens'
title, but two days before the match, with a big house
expected, Stevens suffered a broken cheekbone outside
the ring. It was announced to the public he had suffered
a broken leg while racing motorcycles. Patterson captured the vacant title and held it for an 11 month reign,
downing one babyface after another before the
inevitable showdown with the one person fans thought
was going to master him. The first and most remembered Stevens-Patterson match was on July 11, 1970, an
old-style Texas death match. Stevens, who never lost a
Texas death match in the territory until his send-off in
1971, captured the U.S. title from his rival for the ninth
and what turned out to be the final time, with Haystacks
Calhoun as referee.

At 5'8 1/2" and 225 to 235 pounds, Stevens was short

STEVENS HOLDS TIGHT, BUT DR. BILL CATAPULTS HIM INTO THE ROPES
(1969)

and thick, giving him the appearance of a fireplug. Still, the most noticeable part of his physique, particularly after his late 30s, was his well-earned beer belly. Size was never a detriment in California, as Stevens' ability as a performer and a talker made people believe he could tear up anyone, no matter how big or how imposing they looked. He had a propensity in those days for regularly getting press he wasn't looking for. Trouble in bars, brawls with people who challenged him at the beach, his non-wrestling antics racing and steer wrestling or his troubles with the IRS were often in the news.

Stevens left San Francisco as a regular in 1971 to join the more lucrative AWA, run by Verne Gagne. While Shire's circuit had several more strong years, mainly built around Patterson, it never came close to the level it had achieved with Stevens. After Patterson left for greener pastures in 1977, business fell off and Shire was forced to close it down as a territory in 1979.

Some 20 years after his match with Gomez, after the San Francisco territory he had put on the map had ceased

to exist, Stevens was still the hottest heel in the hottest feud in pro wrestling. He dropped Jimmy Snuka on his head at a WWF television taping in Allentown, PA which led to a series of matches up and down the East Coast that included several major sellouts. These turned Snuka into one of the biggest drawing cards in the world at the time. All in all, Stevens wrestled for 42 years, most of it as a headliner, with his final match just a few years before his death.

He was probably the only headliner whose career started when wrestling was on network television in the early '50s and was still active when it was returned to the networks 33 years later. His career on top started with Gorgeous George. He worked through numerous eras and with many icons world wide – Archie Moore in Atlanta, the Bruiser in Indianapolis, Gene Kiniski in Ohio, Curtis Iaukea in Hawaii, Lewin in Australia, everyone from Bruno on down in California, Gagne and Billy Robinson in the Midwest. He worked all the way to challenging Ric Flair at the Charlotte Coliseum for the NWA title, feuding with Snuka and Bob Backlund in Madison Square Garden and appearing as a dual headliner with Hulk Hogan in

RAY STEVENS BATTLES FORMER WORLD CHAMPION PAT O'CONNOR AT ST. LOUIS' KIEL AUDITORIUM, 1976

the AWA. Perhaps his last main events in a major territory were in the AWA with Nick Bockwinkel, challenging the Road Warriors in 1985 for the AWA tag team titles. He had ceased to be a full-time main event performer in the big money territories shortly after the Snuka run ended. A combination of age, injuries and conditioning had taken its toll, not to mention the oncoming era where steroids and monstrous size ruled the roost and the older and smaller performers, even with legendary names and resumes, appeared out of place. ▶

"God love him. He was still smoking and drinking until the day he went," said Bockwinkel, after learning of his death. "He loved toys. He always had to have the fastest snowmobile, fastest boat, fastest car. He was always upbeat. He was never jealous. If Ray Stevens said a bad word about someone, they obviously deserved it. He was as charitable in the ring as you can get and I learned so much from him."

All his excesses began to catch up with him as he underwent quadruple-bypass surgery at Stanford University after suffering a heart attack while living in Min-

nesota in early 1995. Having spent money as fast as he earned it for most of his wrestling career, he returned to California and moved back in with his first wife. He went right back to his old lifestyle without missing a beat. He was still determined to be Ray Stevens to the end. Apparently even God can't look after those who don't look out for themselves forever.

▶ **Ray Stevens was a main eventer by the** age of 17, when he first made his name in a 1952 feud with Gorgeous George. The matches were promoted by posters with publicity pictures of Stevens wearing a diaper, nicknamed "The Diaper Kid" because he was a heel and very young to be working the main events against the biggest drawing card of the era.

It was in the AWA that he was given the nickname "The Crippler" (the person Paul Heyman patterned his idea for Chris Benoit after), largely based on an angle where he used his "Bombs Away" on Dr. X (Dick Beyer) to break his leg (allowing him to leave on an extended Japanese tour).

Late one Saturday night in 1998, Louie Spicolli was at his home in San Pedro, CA, a beach town suburb of Los Angeles, watching pro wrestling videos with a few friends. His friends started razzing him about how he was looking out of shape. He had stopped going to the gym and he was letting his hair get messy, he explained, because his new WCW character was going to be like Chris Farley. But he told them he was worried, because the drug use by some of his co-workers and friends in the company was starting to scare him, and he was no stranger to the pitfalls of drugs. Ultimately, like far too many others in his profession, he was right. On both counts.

Spicolli was found dead by his friend John Hannah the next morning. Hannah, who stayed over at his house that night, woke up to a really bad odor. When he opened the door to Spicolli's room, he knew right away what had happened. Spicolli was lying face first on the floor, there was vomit all over the place, his ankles were swollen and his body was already discolored. He had turned 27 five days earlier.

Spicolli had taken 26 Somas, a prescription sleeping pill/pain killer that is alleged to be the drug of choice in the wrestling profession today. The drugs are easily obtainable through noted "mark doctors." He combined the pills with wine, apparently the only beverage in the house. He is said to have built up an incredible tolerance for Somas, and would take 15 without it even affecting him. He took 25 to 30 every night before going to bed. He felt he needed them to sleep, but it was a dosage that would hospitalize an average person. He'd wake up fresh the next morning and go to the gym.

On this night, he got to bed at about 2:30 AM. Hannah, sleeping in the next room, recalls being momentar-

ily awakened at 4:15 AM by Spicolli's heavy snoring. He also recalls the alarm clock going off at 5:10 AM, and Spicolli reflexively turning it off. The paramedics were surprised because the state of the body the next morning indicated he'd been dead a lot longer. Hannah was going to wake Spicolli up to get him ready for an early afternoon flight to Tampa for Nitro the next day. The actual cause of death was a heart attack from an enlarged heart. When the police arrived, they theorized that the wine multiplied the effects of the pills by as much as tenfold.

Spicolli, real name Louis Mucciolo, took his ring name from the always-stoned surfer played by Sean Penn in the

LOUIE AS MERCENERIE IN TIJUANA, *RIGHT:* LOUIE SPICOLLI AND OWEN HART, IN CALGARY

LOUIE SPICOLLI AT ECW'S FIRST PPV IN THE OPENING MATCH,
FACING PAGE: LOUIE SPICOLLI VS. CHRIS BENOIT

cult movie classic "Fast Times at Ridgemont High." He had been a big wrestling fan from the age of 14, and was enamored with the World Wrestling Federation during its glory days drawing big houses monthly at the Los Angeles Sports Arena. There is actually a tape of a teenage Lou Mucciolo at ringside in the crowd at Saturday Night's Main Event show taped at the Sports Arena in November of 1986. While attending a show, he met up with ring announcer Bill Laster (Billy Anderson), and began training with him at a garage in East Los Angeles with the Mexican Luchadores when he was just 16 years old. Mucciolo was a natural athlete, a standout high school pitcher with a great arm who was actually believed to have had great potential in that sport. But he never really cared for baseball, or school, or anything but wrestling. He dropped out of high school to follow his dream. His natural athletic ability allowed him to pick things up quickly and after just three months of training, a few days after his 17th birthday, Anderson brought him

as a jobber to a WWF television taping in Bethlehem, PA where he had his first match putting over Ron Bass. Over the next several years, he worked as a WWF jobber, highly regarded enough that he was used not only on local tapings, but flown to wherever the tapings were being held. He was generally considered one of the best jobbers the company had. He continued for several years on and off, until he quit because he knew he'd be typecast. Even in later years he was brought in as an opponent for guys such as Lightning Kid (now Syxx) and Latin Fury (now Konnan) in dark matches at WWF tapings. He also teamed with Anderson and various third members as Los Mercenarios Americanos, a main event foreign heel trio. Working regularly at Auditorio Municipal in Tijuana, holding a version of the World Trios championship, he learned to work against Mexican wrestlers.

In early 1996, while working for the WWF as Rad Radford, after taking about 55 Somas, he was found face-first in a puddle in front of a neighbor's house and was rushed to the hospital. He was in critical condition for two days. At one point he was clinically dead for a few

LOUIE SPICOLLI AND ART BARR BACKSTAGE AT AN AAA SHOW,
FACING PAGE: LOUIE AS WWF'S RAD RADFORD

minutes, and he later talked of smelling the smoke from his deceased grandfather's cigars before the doctors got his heart started again. The WWF wanted to get rid of him immediately. After a lot of public haggling, he was given a full release, after initially being offered a restricted release that wouldn't have allowed him to wrestle for World Championship Wrestling for the duration of his WWF contract.

He had gotten the WWF job after being seen on the AAA When Worlds Collide PPV in November 1994 where, through weights and steroids, he bulked himself up to 265 pounds, always believing that size would get him a job and a push in the WWF. Apparently the WWF had always liked his work, but because of his size, had never

really considered him a serious prospect. However, his work, his newfound weight and his charisma – doing a silly dance under the ring name Madonna's Boyfriend, a gimmick Antonio Pena came up with for him – led to a contract offer literally days after the pay-per-view. Of course, there was a small problem in that he was under an existing contract with Ron Skoler, who promoted the AAA (Asistencia Asesoria y Administracion) shows in the United States, but Skoler let him out of his deal.

After WWF, he wound up in ECW, largely as a favor called in by Sabu, the daredevil who became an underground legend in the mid-90s before injuries caused his star to fade. At first, Spicolli received something of an undercard push getting a big Pavlovian pop by coming out to the famous song, "Louie, Louie." He was the master of the death valley driver, a move he had seen while

LOUIE SPICOLLI WITH THE DEBUTING CHAVO GUERRERO
JR. AND MANDO GUERRERO IN 1994

watching All Japan women wrestlers. But the push stalled over a number of both public and private issues. Spicolli's drug use, which he kept secret except from the boys and a few friends in WWF, was becoming more flagrant. He took as many as 85 Somas in one sitting at his worst. It was not unusual, both in his WWF and ECW days, for him to pass out on airplanes and be taken to emergency rooms to throw it up out of his system. He would miss connecting flights and show up late for shows. It

became bad enough that Paul Heyman considered it a company embarrassment and feared the potential repercussions. Sabu would always back up Spicolli and keep Heyman from getting rid of him. Spicolli, unhappy about his lack of a push and money (he was making about $250 per show), felt that Heyman was making up stories to make him look bad to Sabu and justify getting rid of him.

With relations worsening between the two, Heyman found out that Spicolli had called Bruce Prichard of the WWF trying to broker a deal where he, Sabu and Rob Van

Dam would all leave for the WWF. Heyman claimed to have found out from Kevin Sullivan that Spicolli was trying to get into WCW as well. Spicolli readily admitted to the former but denied the latter. Finally, he quit after getting word that Terry Taylor was getting him a job with WCW. Heyman claimed he had fired him.

He started with WCW at the Orlando television tapings in August, and that job nearly ended right after it started as well. Just a few weeks later he overdosed on Somas again and was hospitalized, but released later that day. Spicolli finally took that as a wake-up call and kicked the pills cold turkey for about a week or two. When he found out that his mother had lymphatic cancer and was only expected to live a few more months, that put him into an emotional tailspin and he started back up. His peer group in WCW made the situation worse. He was mainly used as a television wrestler in WCW, in a glorified jobber role like one of about 30 other wrestlers the company brought in at about the same time. He came up with a new angle. It was basically a comedy gimmick that he suggested to Scott Hall and Hall went to bat for him. He was to be used to put over Larry Zbyszko to keep Hall and Zbyszko's issue going while delaying a second match between the two.

Five days before his death, doing a color routine with Tony Schiavone and Mike Tenay on Nitro, his performance impressed everyone. All of a sudden he was in the plans and there was talk about making him a regular, perhaps as a comedic heel color commentator. He was brought back on Thunder three days later in the same role and was in really good spirits regarding his career coming off his performance on Nitro.

When Spicolli died, the mood in Tampa at Nitro was said to be one of surprise, some sadness, and mostly business. The company did put up a graphic with a picture when the show started, indicating that Spicolli had died. There was no explanation to a viewing audience of millions. Reality, even the harshest kind, can't creep into wrestling television. ▶

FUNERAL CARD FROM LOUIE SPICOLLI'S FUNERAL SERVICE

▶ **In the months before Louie Spicolli's** death, the sport of collegiate wrestling had a major scandal of its own. Three wrestlers died from dehydration due to cutting weight for early season meets. College wrestlers had drastically cut weight as standard operating practice for decades, with occasional dizziness and dehydration but never with fatal consequences. College wrestling responded to this black eye by drastically changing rules as to how much weight a wrestler could cut and changing the time of weigh-ins, basically changing protocol enough that the problem would not be slightly curtailed, but totally eliminated. Professional wrestling handles its problems differently. And reacts much more slowly.

On November 23, 1994 Art "Love Machine" Barr passed away in his sleep at his home in Eugene, OR.

Art Barr had flown back from Mexico City a few days earlier to pick up his five-year-old son Dexter who had spent the weekend with his mother, Gloria Abston. The next day, Abston tried to call the house. When there was no answer, she drove to the house and knocked on the door for an hour. Again there was no answer. At the bedroom window, she saw Art and Dexter both asleep on his waterbed and pounded on the window, waking Dexter, who let her in. She couldn't get Art to awaken, and when medical help arrived, they pronounced him dead, believing he had been dead anywhere from six to 24 hours.

The funeral took place at the Springfield Memorial Gardens and Funeral Home. Besides his immediate family and many wrestlers who worked with him at the Portland Sports Arena, others who attended were Canadian indie workers Buddy Wayne and Michelle Starr, and former wrestlers like Stan Stasiak and Rick Renaldo along with Don Owen and son Barry, whose family ran the old Oregon territory for more than 60 years. Most of the wrestlers wept openly during parts of the service. Ten-bell salutes took place at various EMLL (Empresa Mexicana de la Lucha Libre), AAA and at least one California independent show at the end of the week, with many wrestlers having a hard time controlling their emotions.

Media coverage of the death symbolized in many ways the cultural barriers not only between the United States and Mexico, but between Americans who speak Spanish and English. The death received prominent coverage throughout Mexico. Within the United States, it received coverage on many Spanish language newscasts. There was no English language coverage, except in his home town of Portland, OR. ▶

Art Barr, in his all-too-short life, was a top local cartoon character babyface, a prelim wrestler with a national promotion, a guy who disappeared in his country only to become a headliner and set attendance records for two of the biggest and best-drawing promotions in the world. He was the best heel in the business and a person who changed the style of wrestling. He blended the best of the styles from Mexico, the United States and Japan.

Love Machine was the son of former prelim wrestler Ferrin "Dandy Sandy" Barr. Sandy actually became better known around his home town of Portland for his two decades of service as the referee every Saturday night on "Portland Wrestling," a local institution on Channel 12 Art practically grew up in the Portland Sports Arena, the 2,000-seat converted bowling alley that ran wrestling every Saturday night and once a month for "Tuesday specials." The Sports Arena was his playground. He grew up amidst the wrestling fans, the arena rats and the local television wrestlers, the most famous of whom was his hero, Roddy Piper. At the time, it was thought by narrow-minded promoters in larger and more lucrative territories that Piper, at 210 pounds, was too small to ever make it big.

There were countless others that Barr met as a teenager, from future national superstars like Adrian

▶ **"He was very high on life,"** said Carlos "Konnan" Ashenoff, who met him in WCW in late 1990 and opened the door for him to come to Mexico with EMLL the next year. Ashenoff had come to refer to him as "our Ric Flair." Ron Skoler, who promoted AAA events in the United States, said "I could only give him the highest praise. He had taken great strides to get his personal life in order and had his professional life in order…I think he was going to be the Roddy Piper of the '90s. A Roddy Piper who was a great worker."

ART BARR VS. OCTAGON IN MEXICO

ART BARR VS. SANTO JR., *FACING PAGE:* ART BARR AS THE TAUNTING
BAD GUY HEEL, LOVE MACHINE, IN MEXCIO'S AAA GROUP

Adonis, Curt Hennig and Jimmy Snuka; to local legends like "Playboy" Buddy Rose and Rip "The Crippler" Oliver; to prospects who never quite got there like Ron Starr, Billy Jack Haynes and Tom Zenk; to those who tragedy struck at an early age, like Lonnie "Moondog" Mayne and "Mad Dog" Buzz Sawyer.

Just a few years out of high school, Art got his start in Salem, OR. At 175 pounds, he was a good worker almost from the start but was too small to be taken as a serious wrestler. It was Piper, Barr's mentor, who came up with his first career break. In 1989, Piper told Barr to take his standard ring gear off, changed him into ragged clothes, put white make-up on his face, flour in his hair, and named him "Beetlejuice," after the lead character of a hit movie and children's cartoon series of the same name. "Beetlejuice" became the most popular wrestler in the promotion. He would come out to entrance music leading a procession of kids, ranging from children to teenagers, many dressed up just like him, like a Pied Piper dancing to the ring.

But in July 1989, came the incident that would forever change Barr's life. After a show in Pendelton, OR, Barr was with a 19-year-old wrestling fan named Angela. In the deserted armory, a sexual encounter took place. Barr was later charged with first degree rape. Since Barr had been dancing with young children like a Pied Piper on Saturday night television and his father was a fixture on the show, it turned into more than a rape case. Several reporters were appalled by this accused rapist being portrayed as a hero. The most sizzling newspaper copy probably ever written in the city followed. It never let up.

In July of 1990, the day his trial was to begin, Barr plea-bargained the first degree rape charge down to a first degree sexual abuse charge. During the police investigation, while taking a lie detector test, Barr admitted having sex with the girl and said that he had known at the time she didn't want to have sex with him on a stairway in an empty armory. But he did believe she'd have been willing to have sex with him somewhere else. The girl testified differently – that she never was willing. The outcry only got worse, and the promotion finally

Art Barr vs. the Blue Panther, *facing page:* Art Barr with his partner Eddie Guerrero at New York's Madison Square Gardens — Art's first and only trip to New York. Well-known East Coast valet Destiny is on the left.

World Championship Wrestling at the time was still dueling the World Wrestling Federation fairly equally in adult viewers but was losing the battle in the young children demographic. Jim Herd decided the company needed "Beetlejuice," against the wishes of booker Ole Anderson, who said Barr was "too small" to be a wrestler. Later, when Barr became a superstar, he liked to joke he was the same size as Anderson, only not as fat.

Now with wcw, Barr was "The Juicer" in the same gimmick that got him over in Portland. It was in wcw that he met Charles Ashenoff (Konnan), who had been brought in to form a Mexican tag team in a Pat O'Connor International tag team tournament. Konnan became friends with Barr and after returning to Mexico talked emll promoter Paco Alonso into signing him on as a babyface. So Love Machine, a masked American, was born in March 1991. This was at a time when the wrestling business in Mexico City had caught fire due to the introduction of televised matches. More press followed in Oregon about the sick irony of Art Barr wrestling under a mask in Mexico, using of all names, Love Machine. But pressure couldn't cross the border this time. He could go as far as his ability would take him.

Money and business were great. emll, known by the boys simply as "The Empresa," ran more shows and drew more fans than any wrestling company in the world at the time. Between his guarantee and per-match bonuses for working the extra shots, Love Machine frequently earned in excess of $3,500 a week. Since there was no time to go home, he flew his family down to Mexico to live at the hotel. But they hated it. They wanted to go home and eventually they did. Barr, with no potential job prospects at home, had to stay, taking quick trips home every few weeks.

It was the feud with Blue Panther, the veteran heel, that put Love Machine on the map as a genuine drawing card. They spent months building the feud before setting up a mask vs. mask match for April 3, 1992, at Arena Mexico. Panther defeated Love Machine in front of approximately 18,000 fans packed into the 17,100-seat building. Another 8,000 fans were in the parking lot watching the match on big screens.

One month later, Konnan and Antonio Pena, the

decided to stop using Barr until the heat died down.

At an Oregon boxing and wrestling commission meeting on August 15, 1990, there was talk of revoking Barr's wrestling license based on the guilty plea. While that angle was tricky legally, they did have grounds to deny him a future license. It turned out he had lied on his license application by saying that he had never been convicted of a felony, ignoring a cocaine possession charge he had as a teenager. So he had no license at home, and because of his size, nobody ever believed that he had any potential outside his home territory.

booker, left "The Empresa" to form AAA with the help of Televisa. Panther soon followed, leaving Machine without his leading rival. Behind the scenes, Machine and Pena negotiated a three-year contract that made him one of the highest paid wrestlers in the country to join AAA.

By the end of the year, Barr was finally licensed to wrestle in his native Oregon and returned for a Christmas night tag team tournament where, as the American Love Machine, he and Konnan won the Pacific Northwest tag team titles at the Sports Arena. By this point, the controversy had died out, and there were no media outcries when he was licensed or when he came back, still as a babyface. The belts were taken to Mexico, where they were renamed the AAA world tag team titles.

The famous Juan de la Barrera sellout run followed (13 sellouts in 15 weeks), climaxed by TripleMania, with Machine and Panther continuing to feud. The first major show after TripleMania was July 18, 1993 in Tonala, Jalisco, a suburb of Guadalajara, headlined by Machine's hair vs. Panther's mask. It drew what was believed to have been the all-time record of 20,000 fans for the Guadalajara market. Panther began the match as a heel, although he always had his share of support, and Machine started as a face. Sometime in the third fall that changed. One look. One cocky smirk. That's all it took. After six years of playing babyface, Love Machine had found his professional calling. While Machine lost that match via disqualification for using the dreaded tombstone piledriver, and had his head shaved while Panther went out on a stretcher, he had just found the key to real superstardom. One month later, Eddy Guerrero and El Hijo del Santo were partners in a trios match with Machine on the other team. Machine unmasked Santo, put the mask on, and started beating up Guerrero. Guerrero then turned on the real Santo after Machine gave him his mask back. The next week, Guerrero formed a team with Machine, and the Gringo Locos were born.

The Gringo Locos literally changed the style of Mexican wrestling. Guerrero introduced more of the New Japan, stiffer offensive style and suplexes, while Machine introduced American-style heel big bumps in the ring, and Ric Flair style chops. Combining this with the Mexican high spot style and an incredible array of facial expressions, and with other younger wrestlers quickly emulating then, they took Lucha Libre to the next level. The two almost immediately became the top tag team in Mexico.

Outside the ring, the year wasn't a run of four-star matches every week. Barr's marriage, which survived the pressures of the publicity from the rape charge, the job changes, the wrestling lifestyle and the phone calls from hotel rooms in Mexico, finally unraveled.

Love Machine's last match took place on November 6, 1994 in Los Angeles, and stole the show on the When Worlds Collide PPV. Originally on the card, it was revamped before the show and he was taken off. After much lobbying and his agreement to have his head shaved, the planned Santo vs. Guerrero singles mask vs. hair match turned into the double mask vs. double hair match on pay-per-view. It was one of the best matches that year in the United States. Machine really wanted to wrestle on the show. He wanted it badly enough to agree to lose his hair at a bargain price of $7,500 plus bonuses based on gate and buy rate. He was well aware of just how good he had become, and that few outside Mexico knew it and this was his chance to show it. There was nobody more focused on leaving no stone unturned to have the best match of his life. A few days before the match, he was so excited he could hardly wait. This was going to be the hardest show in the country to steal but he and Guerrero were going to steal it.

A few weeks earlier in Japan, Chris Benoit and Shinjiro Otani screwed up a move they'd planned to debut as the finisher in the New Japan Junior Heavyweight tag team tournament, where Guerrero was on Pegasus' shoulders and Otani was to come off the top rope with a Frankensteiner. Otani couldn't maneuver his weight correctly in mid-air and the move didn't come off as planned. Machine and Guerrero decided they would debut the move on the pay-per-view and get it right. Which they did.

People could no longer dismiss him because he was only 5'10" and 200 pounds, or because his fame was as an American flag-draped heel in Mexico. And finally, within his profession he had something in his present, and no longer his past, that he would immediately be associated with.

Probably from the moment Eddie Gilbert was old enough to understand just what it was that his father did for a living, he was determined to follow in his footsteps. He set his goal as being like his hero, Jerry Lawler, a local wrestling legend, and a booker, before the age of 30.

As a teenager, he would book mock cards, finishes and long-term programs. He was so set on his goals that wrestling became his entire life. He knew exactly where he was going. One day he'd occupy the spot Lawler held and that Jackie Fargo held before him, being the "King" of Channel 5 wrestling, the top draw in the territory, the booker and the perennial champion knocking off the big names from other territories weekly in Memphis, Louisville and the rest of the circuit.

Eddie Gilbert achieved his first two goals. It was doubtful he'd ever achieve the third one. He embarked on a course of self-destruction that led him to Puerto Rico and a demise not too many miles from where another of his childhood heroes, Bruiser Brody, was killed. He lived, ate, drank and slept wrestling, and when things didn't go his way, he took it out on those closest to him, alienated many of his best friends, and tragically became a statistic in the bizarre saga of second-generation wrestlers.

Gilbert, who was booking the Puerto Rican based World Wrestling Council (wwc), was found dead in his apartment in Isla Verde, Puerto Rico on a Saturday night in February of 1995, at approximately 6:30 PM by veteran wrestler Ken Wayne (Ken Peale). The two were scheduled to meet at 10 AM that morning to go over finishes for the show that night and booking ideas for the future, but when Wayne came to his room, there was no answer at the door. Finally, when it was time for them to leave for a

show that evening in nearby Trujillo Alto, Wayne, who had arrived in Puerto Rico only eight days earlier, broke in through a window. He found a limp Gilbert across the bed, with his feet badly swollen. When Karl Moffat, the original Jason the Terrible from Calgary, who was living downstairs in the same complex, came in to check for a pulse, he found out what Wayne knew almost immediately. The person who had phoned him at home ten days earlier, who he had known for more than twenty years, well before either had gotten started in the business, was dead at the age of 33. The doctor who examined the body said the death was due to a heart attack, which probably occurred at some point while he was asleep the previous night. The autopsy credited the heart attack as being caused by a cocaine overdose.

Gilbert had started as booker for Carlos Colon after walking out of Smoky Mountain Wrestling (smw). Gilbert's reputation for walking out on promotions was so well established that it was only the dearth of experi-

EDDIE "KING" GILBERT AND PAUL E., *RIGHT:* EDDIE WITH HIS FATHER, TOMMY GILBERT

GILBERT IN THE UWF WITH TERRY TAYLOR, BEING INTERVIEWED BY JIM ROSS.
FACING PAGE: EDDIE GILBERT AFTER A BOUT

enced talent that could viably work as headliners in the smaller promotions and a reputation as a creative booker that had kept his career alive the last few years of his life. He had walked out in Memphis, his home territory, so many times nobody could even keep track. Lawler would always take him back because he was a good, often great worker with excellent ring psychology and he did entertaining interviews.

Gilbert and Wayne worked in Humacao a few weeks before his death. Gilbert was the promotion's top heel, wrestling a live wrestling bear. It was a throwback to a long-forgotten wrestling gimmick from Gilbert's childhood. Top heels would be "tricked" into getting in the ring with bears and do panic-laden interviews, which often drew a good house.

During his 17-year career, Gilbert had wrestled at one time or another for most major offices around the world and gained a reputation for being a very good worker, but

being undersized for the role as top heel. He had been told so many times that he was good enough but not big enough to headline that he was constantly worried about his weight. That in turn led him to steroids. In the last years of his life he became well-known for his creative and sometimes erratic booking. Starting in 1987 with Bill Watts' UWF, he was also an assistant for Dusty Rhodes in Jim Crockett's NWA, briefly turning around a dying Alabama territory. That won him the 1988 Booker of the Year award. He resurfaced as part of the booking committee for WCW, and later was booker in Memphis, Puerto Rico, Global in Texas and for ECW. He generally left on bad terms at every stop. He did interviews on live television, left territories with the title belts, and even double-crossed promoters in the ring on his way out.

"He was raised in an environment where he learned never to believe anyone," said ECW promoter Ted Gordon. "So he lived his life paranoid of everyone and everything." Not only was Eddie Gilbert's father a long-time star in Tennessee, best known as being tag team partner of Eddie

GILBERT IN A BLOODY I-QUIT MATCH WITH ONE OF HIS MENTORS AND IDOLS, TERRY FUNK, *FACING PAGE:* "HOT STUFF" EDDIE GILBERT

Marlin in the '60s and '70s, but his grandfather used to wrestle in the carnivals. He had gotten into writing and taking pictures at wrestling events, often alongside another teenager from Louisville named Jim Cornette.

His first angle was as part of a father and son tag team feuding with Ken Wayne and father Buddy Wayne. He then went to work for Bob Geigel in Kansas City as a protege of Bulldog Bob Brown and got work in opening matches for Sam Muchnick in St. Louis when it was considered the top wrestling city in the country.

Gilbert and his father then ventured into Leroy McGuirk's Oklahoma version of the old Championship Wrestling territory after Bill Watts had taken over the Louisiana end of McGuirk's former five-state territory in 1980. He returned to Tennessee toward the end of the

year and by early 1981 started tag teaming with the son of another local wrestling personality, Ricky Morton. He was part of the most memorable matches of the '80s and a videotape collectors all-time classic, the 1981 Tupelo, MS concession stand brawl against Atsushi Onita and Masa Fuchi. Morton and Gilbert went back to McGuirk's territory in its dying days, at which point he and his father ventured to Puerto Rico as a tag team.

Gilbert had met Vince McMahon Sr. at an NWA convention and Sr. invited him to come to the Northeast in 1982. Since Gilbert was much smaller than most wrestlers in the big-man territory, he was the prime opponent later when the original Tiger Mask (Satoru Sayama) was brought into the WWF for a few tours. Perhaps the turning point of his career came in 1983 while driving back from a television taping. He got into a major auto accident which resulted in a broken neck. While the original word was that his career would be over, he

GILBERT WITH THE LEGENDARY KILLER KOWALSKI

▶ Most ex-wrestlers who were promoters in that era built the territory around men much like themselves. Tennessee was an extension of Jerry Jarrett, small guys often with no physiques whatsoever, wild matches and angles, young bleached-blond babyfaces who would juice frequently to gain sympathy from the young women fans. Eddie Gilbert was a tailor-made mid-card wrestler in that system. AWA was an extension of Verne Gagne, lots of former amateur wrestlers, many of them very old, or old ex-football players. Leroy McGuirk, a former junior heavyweight champion and top collegian, used smaller guys with good wrestling backgrounds. Watts, a 300-pounder who played football and wrestled in college (although neither as successfully as his later legend would attest to), liked big, strong ex-jocks on the face side – Steve Williams or Jim Duggan being the prototype – and even bigger foreign or anti-American heels. When Bill Dundee came in and the company started drawing money with smaller babyfaces, Watts tempered his position on the face side.

returned to wrestling in Tennessee just a few months later and eventually returned to the WWF as the protege of then-champion Bob Backlund. When The Masked Superstar (Bill Eadie) came into the WWF and used a reverse neckbreaker to "re-injure" Gilbert, it set up a series of Backlund-Superstar matches, where a white-coated Dr. George Zahorian would pronounce Gilbert re-injured after each match.

In 1984, he left WWF and returned to Tennessee teaming with Tommy Rich as The New Fabulous Ones. Stan Lane and Steve Keirn had become one of the hottest acts in the history of the territory as The Fabulous Ones, billed as proteges of local legend "Fabulous" Jackie Fargo. When the two went to work for the AWA, they left a big hole and caused attendance to drop. The promotion had Fargo say on television that Stan and Steve had gotten too big and didn't want to wrestle in Memphis anymore and instead wanted to go to New York and Chicago, but he was bringing in a tag team the local fans could be proud of. When it became obvious that they were thought of as

copies of one of the most popular acts ever to appear in the area, Gilbert agreed to turn heel on Rich and in doing so established himself for the first time as a headliner.

In 1985 he left Tennessee for Bill Watts' Mid South Wrestling, a group that turned itself around doing big business using ex-Memphis undercard guys like Ricky Morton, Robert Gibson, Terry Taylor, Jim Cornette, Bobby Eaton and Dennis Condrey in strong positions. ▶

The idea of a guy 5'8 1/2" and 200 pounds as a top heel was something Bill Watts wasn't ready for, even though he took a liking to Gilbert. Gilbert started as a jobber at UWF, and was shifted over to a managerial role. Finally he was used as almost a coach for larger men like The Blade Runners (later Sting and Ultimate Warrior) and Rob Rechsteiner (later Rick Steiner). Gilbert came up with enough unique angles and was a strong enough worker that he worked his way up the shows, and eventually, when Watts was already making noises about getting out of wrestling, he gave Gilbert his life-long goal. He made him booker. Gilbert shot an angle with himself to turn Sting babyface, telling everyone who would listen

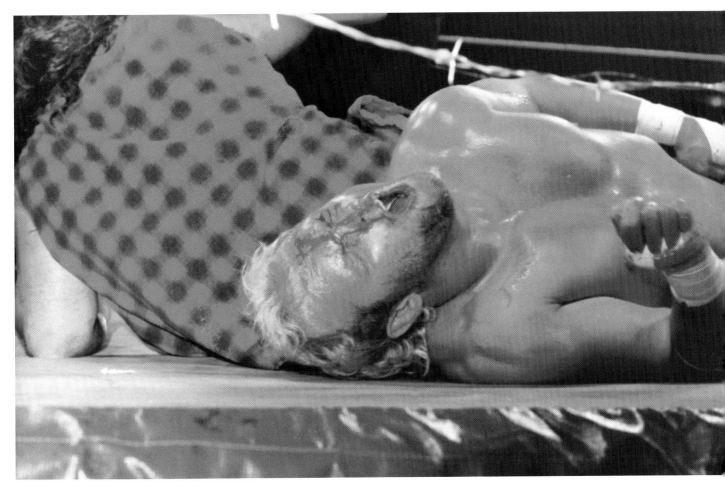

one year before anyone else figured it out that Sting would be the next major superstar in wrestling. He also started out Shane Douglas, who he saw while working an independent show in Ohio, giving him his name and his first push, claiming he was also a future superstar.

Watts' company was on its last legs and there was probably nothing anyone could have done to save it, but when he sold the company to Crockett, it put Gilbert on TBS for the first time. That relationship quickly disintegrated when he felt the UWF wrestlers were getting buried to put over the NWA wrestlers.

There is a lot that can be said about Eddie Gilbert. He was not unique among wrestlers, but was something of an exception. He cared more than most about his own personal performance. He would have rather worked smaller shows on top and have control over his character and ring performance than work for the big companies and be held back. He was a more creative booker than many, if not most.

There is also a lot that can be learned from him. Most people who knew him will remember that he was a very good, sometimes great performer who had an unusual love for and intelligence regarding pro wrestling. That he could be a very charming person. That he started out as a wrestling fan, even though he grew up as a part of the business because of his father, and remained a fan and close to many fans while in the business. And that he had a serious drug problem. We can't say that Gilbert died specifically from drugs, but the drugs certainly didn't help. Taking steroids while having high blood pressure is no way to avoid a heart attack.

When Gilbert died, the USWA (United States Wrestling Association), his hometown promotion; ECW, and SMW, the last promotion in the United States he worked for, all held ceremonies in the ring at matches to honor him. Both USWA and ECW also did television video tributes. Several independent shows, including some in places as far away as the weekly Calgary Friday night Canadian Rocky Mountain wrestling show, ran in-ring tributes as well.

Sammy Steamboat was wrestling Professor Boris "The Great" Malenko on the syndicated Championship Wrestling from Florida television show, when Malenko began biting Steamboat's ear and there was heavy juice. For that part of the country and that time period, it was particularly gruesome, especially for television. Eddie Graham, the promoter and top babyface, came to the desk where announcer Gordon Solie was and said he was going to have to stop the match and take drastic measures to do so. Graham hit the ring attacking Malenko, then punched him and Malenko's false teeth flew out of his mouth. Graham then began stomping Malenko's teeth into oblivion.

With the exception of the 1974 angle when Pak Song and Gary Hart turned on partner Dusty Rhodes at the famed Fort Homer Hesterly Armory in Tampa, this is probably the most well remembered angle in the history of Florida wrestling. Although there was virtually no communication across territory lines in those days as it was largely a secretive business, it was one of the few angles that was famous within pro wrestling all over the world.

Malenko, real name Larry Simon, was one of the top heels and best interviews in pro wrestling during the '60s and later one of the most well-known wrestling trainers in the world. His death in September of 1994, which was not unexpected, came from an infection due to his weakened condition from rigorous chemotherapy treatments for leukemia.

Many credit Malenko with being the wrestler most responsible for originally popping Graham's Florida territory, which in the '70s was regarded nationwide as probably the best wrestling territory in the country. Billed as both the inventor and the master of the Russian chain

MALENKO AND MASKED SUPERSTAR, WHO BORIS MANAGED FOR A WHILE. HAMPTON COLISEUM, 1974 OR 1975

match, he was also a major drawing card in many other territories in the southern United States and also in Australia. ▶

"He knew how to manipulate fans," remembered his son Dean. "And he knew it took patience to get yourself established. When I was growing up, we had to change the tires on our car almost every day. We had rocks thrown through our windows, death threats. That was his applause. Every old territory was built on the heel and there are no true heels anymore."

Sometimes he manipulated fans too well. War stories old wrestlers tell of Malenko are exactly that. Wrestling as German Otto Von Krupp for the Dusek family in Nebraska, whom he credited with giving him his real education in pro wrestling in the late '50s, he stirred up fans to the point of riot on numerous occasions and was known for having to fight his way out of buildings. It was ironic that a Jewish man from New Jersey was playing a

---

▶As a trainer, Larry Malenko, as he was known in later years, helped start out wrestlers like Johnny B. Badd, 1–2–3 Kid, Paul Diamond, Typhoon, Chris Champion, Barry Horowitz, Al and Lou Perez, his sons Joe and Dean, Brady Boone, Timothy Well, Bobby Blaze, Ricky Santana, Buddy Landel, The Black Hearts, and several women wrestlers including Debbie Malenko (no relation). He helped put additional touches on training for numerous other wrestlers in the formative stages of their career, like Rick Steamboat and Bill Eadie. He was also involved in the late '80s in booking foreign talent for the old UWF (Universal Wrestling Federation) when it was the hottest promotion in the world.

"He was the most believable heel I ever saw," said Steve Beverly, who grew up watching Malenko as the top heel Thursday nights during the mid-'60s.

MALENKO IN ACTION DURING A MATCH WITH PAUL JONES. RICHMOND
COLISEUM, 1973

post-war German in Nebraska. One of the most famous
riots ever in the Carolinas took place in the mid-'60s
involving Malenko under his Russian guise with tag partner Bob Orton Sr. against the Flying Scott Brothers,
George and Sandy Scott.

"I was a hayseed from Kansas with a blond crewcut
as Southern heavyweight champion (when Eddie Gra-

ham tried to expand his top regional title in Florida into
other NWA promotions)," remembered Orton. "I was
teaming up with a Russian. You talk about heat. The fans
thought I was a traitor teaming with a Russian. We went
into Raleigh. George Becker was the booker. They were
running a building and doing one-quarter houses. He
(Malenko) got on television one time and all he did was
smash a chain onto a chair. We almost sold out. But we

had too much heat. Tom Renesto wanted us to hold it down. We tried to calm things down but the more we tried, the hotter it got."

Things exploded in a match near Richmond when the fans overpowered and trampled the minimal security that was hired, and Malenko was slashed by a knife-wielding fan and needed 33 stitches in the abdomen. Orton was knocked out by a chair and trampled on. The heat was so strong, Orton immediately left the territory, returned to Florida and turned babyface.

Although Malenko wrestled virtually everywhere – from Australia to Japan to almost every U.S. territory – aside from his success in Florida, his biggest runs were in the Carolinas and in Texas. Malenko was a major draw opposite both Fritz Von Erich and Wahoo McDaniel, culminating in a Russian chain match with McDaniel at the Astrodome in Houston for promoter Paul Boesch. The match set what was at the time the city's all-time attendance record.

The Florida promotion, originally run by Cowboy Luttrell, was a seasonal company that would shut down every summer because they believed no money could be made. By the early '60s, the decision was made to run year-round. Malenko was the first heel to consistently sellout arenas opposite Graham, starting in 1963. After that he went to the Carolinas with Orton as a team. After the riot, Orton returned to Florida as Southern champ, teaming with former rival Graham. From the Carolinas, Malenko said in interviews that he was shocked that his friend and former partner could ever team with Graham. Upon his return, Malenko and Missouri Mauler (Larry Hamilton, older brother of Assassin #2 Jody Hamilton) feuded with Graham and Orton, and did another run of packed houses.

The heel run that made him famous came after the false teeth angle. As the angle continued, the NWA ordered Graham to pay Malenko for his false teeth. Graham said he'd never pay for Malenko's teeth and was then suspended. He left the territory for two months, returning once under a mask, claiming to be the Lone Ranger. It was several months before he was reinstated and came back, with the rematches drawing what were then record crowds in almost every city the two would appear in. Although Graham won many of their chain

matches, Malenko became billed as the man who had never lost a Russian chain match and he would fly into other NWA territories during a time when few wrestlers were flown into cities and work with the local hero (who in those days was usually also the owner or booker of the company) with the chain gimmick. He remained the top heel in Florida.

The heel run ended in the summer of 1971 when Jack and Jerry Brisco and Tim Woods defeated Malenko, Dick Murdoch and Rene Goulet on a Tuesday night in Tampa due to a miscue among the heel threesome. They tagged up two days later at the television tapings where Murdoch and Goulet turned on him, setting up another run of big houses when Malenko put up $5,000 to Graham as a promise not to turn on him and be his tag partner to get revenge. He was a key face in the promotion for several years, feuding with the likes of Bobby Shane, Buddy Colt and Dusty Rhodes (then a heel), usually culminating in chain matches, which he always won. Then a falling out with Championship Wrestling from Florida ended his career with the company that he helped put over the top and that put him over the top.

Exactly what happened was unclear.

"Eddie and Larry had a falling out," remembered Phyllis Lee, a long-time friend of Malenko's. "Eddie claimed Larry used a company ticket to take his wife to the Bahamas. Larry denied it. The boys said that Eddie was afraid because Larry was getting more popular than him. Eddie had Larry blackballed by the NWA. For years Hiro (Matsuda), Duke (Keomuka) and Gordon Solie (who ran the company along with Graham) wouldn't even talk to him. Finally Gordon came. It took a long time to get Larry to even talk to Gordon. Finally Hiro came."

When Malenko was blacklisted by the NWA, he started running in competition in the Tampa area. The heat was such that other NWA promoters would send their top talent to Florida for Graham's shows to run head-to-head where Malenko was running shows. Malenko's friends joked that even though they didn't ultimately win the war, they did score the major public relations victory. The heat was such that Dusty Rhodes, then the company's top face, in a television interview on the wrestling show started bad-mouthing Malenko and his group. Malenko, who was considered a tough guy who always kept himself in great shape and had some training with Henry Wittenberg (a gold medalist in the 1948 Olympics), responded challenging Rhodes to a match with all the proceeds going to charity. He even had his sons, Joe and Dean, who were both just getting started in wrestling but were trained by Karl Gotch in shooting which made them feared in the business, challenge Mike and Eddie Graham. That immediately shut everyone's mouth at CWF.

A native of Irvington, NJ, Larry Simon started wrestling under his real name for Vince McMahon Sr. in the early '50s. He later worked as Larry Dugan and Crusher Dugan before going to Nebraska and Missouri for the Duseks and Gust Karras as Otto Von Krupp. After returning to the Northeast under his real name, McMahon gave him the Malenko name, which he never used in the Northeast.

Malenko was known for his physical conditioning. Orton compared him, at 5'10", 260 pounds at his largest (although during most of his career he weighed in the 230 range), to a Road Warrior. He had a unique way of walking with one eye closed and another open, while the babyface would make comebacks on him. But above all, he was most well-known for his interviews. Many of his contemporaries rated him behind only King Curtis Iaukea as the best interview in the business during the '60s.

"Guys like Terry Funk would play tapes of my dad," said his son, Dean. "My dad talked very slow. Slow, methodical interviews. When he did an interview, you wanted to buy a ticket for Tuesday night."

"He was very unique. He wasn't as big as Bruno, but he studied and understood what it took to draw money. Hulk Hogan, Slater, Beefcake all grew up watching him at the armory. Terry (Bollea) can recite word-for-word some of his interviews."

In 1978 and 1979, Malenko had his final run as an active wrestler for Southeastern Championship Wrestling in Knoxville. He re-did the false teeth angle, this time with Ronnie Garvin. Also in the late '70s he went back to the Carolinas when George Scott was booking, as the manager of The Masked Superstar (Eadie) and Kim Duk, before returning home to Florida and getting the wrestling school going. In the Carolinas he was involved in a relatively famous angle as well, where he used his lit cigar to burn the eyes of the Mighty Igor. ▶

▶ **Several hundred people attended Larry Malenko's funeral in Tampa. Many were major** industry names including Matsuda, Steve Keirn, Solie, Cyclone Negro, Stu Schwartz (a former referee in Florida), George Scott, Don Curtis, 1–2–3 Kid, Randy (Savage), Lanny and Angelo Poffo, Masao Hattori (New Japan referee-booker, a world class amateur in the early '70s who was Dean's amateur wrestling coach), Karl Gotch, Koji Kanemoto, Osamu Nishimura and numerous others. Hans Mortier, one of his best friends, flew in from Holland and spent several weeks with him in the hospital during his first round of chemotherapy, while others like John Tolos and Bruno Sammartino kept in constant telephone communication with him during his last few months.

It wasn't anyone in wrestling, but someone Dean had never met, who hit home that day. "A guy drove down from Tallahassee. He never met us but came up to me and told me how my father brought a lot of happiness to him and his family. It really got to me."

Montreal newspapers reported that dealings with contraband cigarettes were the reason for the mob-style retaliation murder of long-time pro wrestling star Dino Bravo.

Bravo, 44, real name Adolfo Bresciano, was shot seven times and killed sometime on the evening of March 10, 1993 in his home in a luxurious section of Laval, Quebec, a city 20 minutes north of Montreal. Laval police found 17 shells from semi-automatic .22 and .380 caliber guns on the floor of Bravo's living room. Because there were no signs of a struggle or forced entry, police believed Bravo knew his killers. Both Bravo's wife and 6-year-old daughter were out for the evening at a ballet class. Bravo's wife, Diane Rivest, last talked to her husband at 9 PM that evening. When she arrived home with their daughter at 12:20 AM, she found her husband dead sitting on his easy chair with the television on. Because there were so many shots fired, including one which broke a window, and because none of his neighbors heard anything, it caused speculation that the killers were professionals who may have used silencers. Police also found a large sum of money in his home.

Le Journal, a Montreal French language newspaper, headlined Bravo's death on the front page with a heading which translated into "Dino Bravo executed for trafficking in tobacco." A full-page story ran on page three of the newspaper in which police refused to confirm that their investigation was focusing on contraband cigarettes as a reason for his murder. However, a follow-up quoted an officer from Longueuil, a city 20 minutes south of Montreal where the RCMP (Royal Canadian Mounted Police) had seized 234 cases of cigarettes and 69 cases of tobacco worth $400,000 on the black market,as saying, "A $400,000 loss of money in importing cigarettes is enough to justify an assassination." Another officer reported that the police believed "it was a settling of

accounts." Laval police, who put 12 men on the case full-time, were tight-lipped. RCMP investigators say they saw Bravo with well-known traffickers but his role in the trafficking couldn't be proven. It was speculated he hadn't covered his tracks well enough, which led to the major bust.

The story said that Bravo had become involved in smuggling cigarettes after he left pro wrestling in 1991, although others trace his involvement back further. The RCMP confirmed Bravo's significant involvement in the operation. The newspaper also reported that Bravo had confided to friends that he didn't think he had long to live. Gino Brito, a long-time friend, tag team partner and business partner of Bravo's, did say in *La Presse*, another French paper that he had heard rumors Bravo's life had been threatened, although he admitted the two had kept their distance from one another during the final months of Bravo's life. Bravo had also been involved in the local boxing scene since the end of his wrestling career.

La Presse also reported Bravo had been an acquaintance of many who were arrested the week before his death, when the RCMP seized 477 kilos of cocaine smuggled into Montreal in tomato cans.

In Canada for a time in the early to mid '90s, the federal government had high duties and taxes on cigarettes manufactured locally, and smuggling became a huge business. Some say it was even more lucrative than hardcore drugs. Smuggling American cigarettes from the Northeast into Quebec and selling them at a much cheaper price than domestic cigarettes from car trunks and fly-by-night warehouses was apparently Bravo's business.

Within wrestling, it was often rumored that Bravo's name was linked to the Montreal underworld. His aunt Maria was the wife of Vic Cotroni, who had a reputation for being Montreal's leading mob godfather. Bravo often

worked as chauffeur for Paul Cotroni, a relative of Vic's who was reportedly a member of the powerful underworld family. Rumors only got stronger when Gino Brito, his partner in several businesses including the local regional wrestling office, was arrested as part of a loan sharking ring.

Bravo began wrestling in his native Montreal in 1970. He began amateur wrestling at the age of 15 and was studying law at Sir George Williams College in Montreal when be became best friends with Yvon Robert Jr. His hero growing up was Yvon Robert, a former NWA champion who for years was the most popular wrestler in Montreal. He was trained at The Grand Prix Wrestling training school by Edouard Carpentier, Luigi Macera and Brito. Because of his strength, he was pushed from the start as part of a young Italian babyface tag team combination with Brito, who was already a star wrestler. Although the two were billed as cousins during their wrestling days, they actually weren't related. After one year he was so high on the cards that he often joined Jean Ferre (André the Giant) and Carpentier on top in six-mans.

Bravo toured many of the American circuits during the '70s and early '80s, getting a strong babyface push holding tag team titles, usually with another Italian wrestler like Dom DeNucci, Tony Parisi, or Brito as an Italian connection tag team. In Southern California, which was his first major campaign after leaving Montreal, he held the tag team title with Victor Rivera. He often returned to Montreal, a bigger star on each return trip, then would venture to another American territory for a six-month campaign. When Eddie Einhorn's IWA bucked the established U.S. offices in its ill-fated '70s promotion, Bravo and Brito were a mid-level tag team which was his first exposure in the Northeast. Soon after, Bravo was in the WWWF. He was given a major singles push, but ended up teaming with DeNucci in 1978 and held the WWWF tag team title, winning the titles from Professor Tanaka and Mr. Fuji, then losing them to the Yukon Lumberjacks (Zarnoff LeBeouff of Montreal and the late Scott Irwin).

At about 240 pounds, Bravo combined the tag team flying maneuvers that young babyfaces were expected to use in the '70s, with impressive strength. He was pushed as being able to bench press in excess of 500 pounds.

AT THE NORFOLK SCOPE AGAINST MASKED SUPERSTAR AND KIM DUK, THE KOREAN ASSASSIN, NORFOLK, VIRGINIA, 1975

When he returned full-time to Montreal around 1981, he, Brito, Tony Mule, and Frank Valois joined forces to form International Wrestling, which became Quebec's major wrestling promotion. Since Carpentier had been removed from the top, the decision was made to go with Bravo as the group's top star along with Quebec City's Rick Martel. The group ran every Monday at Paul Sauve Arena in Montreal drawing respectable to very good crowds in the medium-sized building. Bravo held the group's international title more often than not and brought in many of the biggest names in the business to challenge for it, drawing crowds in excess of 10,000 for the major shows at the Montreal Forum. Among the top heel names Bravo brought in to challenge for his title

BRAVO BRINGS MASKED SUPERSTAR TO THE MAT AS THE KOREAN ASSASSIN
LOOK ON AT THE NORFOLK SCOPE, 1975

were Abdullah the Butcher (probably his most frequent major adversary), The Road Warriors, Samu, Pat Patterson, Haku, Ric Flair, Rick Valentine (Kerry Brown) and Leo Burke. ▶

Bravo first came to the WWF as a babyface in 1985 with a minimal push, although he always headlined the Montreal shows. He left the promotion in 1986 after a strange incident. A WWF show was held in the Forum on January 15, 1986. The main event on the show was billed as Hulk Hogan defending the title against Bravo, who was the most popular local wrestling name. The show drew a sellout of nearly 20,000, but the card was re-arranged the night of the show with Hogan and Bravo each wrestling different opponents, apparently because WWF officials were worried that Hogan would be perceived as the heel against the local French-speaking star.

Bravo returned in 1987, and became a bleached-blond heel for the first time in his career and tag team partner of Greg Valentine. Later he teamed with Earthquake in 1990-91, as a top of the card heel working many main event tag team matches against Hulk Hogan and

▶ **International Wrestling was one of the** many regional companies that folded when confronted with competition from the WWF, the key blow being when the WWF signed The Rougeau Brothers. After that the other top local draws, Bravo and Martel, wound up with the WWF and eventually Titan made Brito its local promoter, a position he held until he disappeared from the Montreal wrestling scene after his much publicized arrest.

Tugboat. He got occasional title shots at Hogan in what seemed like one of the most curious main event pushes in wrestling. ▶

Bravo worked full-time with the wwf through Wrestlemania of 1991. After that, he worked in Puerto Rico on top against Carlos Colon, and did fill-in duty for the wwf. He also worked some shows in Montreal, working as a face in his home town once again. His final wwf action is believed to have been the April 1992 European tour. He was scheduled for a well publicized retirement match on December 4, 1992, at the Montreal Forum on the wwf show. But several weeks before the card, at roughly the same time as Brito's arrest, the wwf pulled Bravo from the card.

▶ **On a national basis, Bravo is probably** best remembered for his farcical attempt at breaking the world record in the bench press during the first Royal Rumble in January 1988 from Hamilton, Ontario. Bravo easily pressed weights billed from 450 to 660 pounds, although the weights themselves were gimmicked. He then attempted to press what was billed as 710 pounds (the world record held at the time by Ted Arcidi, himself a one-time pro wrestler, was 705) but "failed" and needed help from spotter Jesse Ventura. After that, Bravo was billed as Canada's strongest man in his heel role. While he was considered a decent worker who was fairly agile and acrobatic during the '70s, he gained about 20 pounds and slowed down considerably in the ring during the period he gained the most fame. His best work no doubt by that time was in the weight room.

DINO BRAVO HELD MANY REGIONAL TITLES, MAINLY IN MONTREAL

Tomomi Tsuruta, who started out as an instant sensation and went on to be one of the most enduring stars in pro wrestling history, passed away in May 2000 from complications after undergoing a kidney transplant operation in the Philippines. He was 49.

Tomomi Tsuruta was an undisputable Hall of Fame calibre performer. He was a major star in pro wrestling literally from the first week of his career in Japan. He was the country's first truly elite-level world-class worker, and was still arguably the best in the business at the time he first took ill. In wrestling, he was known for nearly three decades by one word, "Jumbo." It was a nickname chosen for him in a contest sponsored by NTV (Nippon Television Network) in Japan a few weeks after his debut in the country after being a celebrated amateur wrestler. He was the first wrestler to hold the Triple Crown, the first native Japanese wrestler to capture the AWA world heavyweight title, and in the late '70s was under somewhat serious consideration to hold the NWA world heavyweight title, which at the time was the major belt in the wrestling world.

Press coverage in Japan called Tsuruta the strongest wrestler in the history of Japanese wrestling. In polls for both the decade of the '80s and '90s, fans voted Tsuruta as the strongest native wrestler.

During the '70s, Tsuruta was considered right at the top of any list of the best workers of the decade. His name always appeared alongside the likes of The Funks, Harley Race and Jack Brisco with a believable high spot athletic style that was ahead of its time. His matches still hold up well under today's standards. He was the first Japanese wrestler to be a world-class worker at a mixture of both American and Japanese styles, having trained

under Dory Funk Jr. and having classic matches with the top scientific wrestlers of the era like Brisco, Funk, Billy Robinson, Race, Nick Bockwinkel, Mil Mascaras and Verne Gagne. These matches aired on prime time network television every Saturday night making him a sports celebrity. He remained a main-eventer throughout the '80s. The emergence of a new, faster-paced style culminating in many near falls, combined with advancing age and increasing size left him somewhat behind the top few guys in the business. By the late '80s and early '90s, he modernized his style to keep up with the pack, and his matches against the likes of Mitsuharu Misawa, Toshiaki Kawada, Genichiro Tenryu and Kenta Kobashi were the state-of-the-art for in-ring world title matches at the time. By that point, he was ranked with the likes of Jushin Liger and Ric Flair as the best in-ring performer in the business, and was the dominant player in the hottest promotion in the world.

Then, just as suddenly, his career, at least as a serious performer, was over. He became ill in the summer of 1992. It was said to have been an ankle injury, but when he came back to the ring six weeks later, he had lost a lot of weight, mainly muscle mass, and clearly was not the same. His stamina was no longer there and tag team partner Akira Taue had to carry the action in his matches, which were still headlining the shows. A few months later, he disappeared again. His illness was never explained to the public. He didn't return to the ring until 11 months later, at which time it was said he had been out of action from contracting Hepatitis B. From that point on, his wrestling was limited to appearing in mid-card six-man tag team matches where he'd only be in for a minute or less at a time. While he wrestled five to ten matches per year over the next five years, the Jumbo Tsuruta that every wrestling fan in Japan knew really was finished in 1992. He left Japan in the fallout from the death of Shohei Baba in early 1999 and began teaching physical education at the University of Portland. He took a turn for the worse toward the end of the year, due to cancer, which was kept secret.

Tomomi Tsuruta was born March 25, 1951 in the small town of Makioka in the Yamanishi Prefecture of Japan. Because his first name sounded so much like Tomoko, a popular first name for girls, he was teased greatly, but grew up to be an excellent athlete. At Hikawa High School, he was a star on the swimming team, was the star player on his high school basketball team which won the Japanese high school national championship during his senior year in 1970, and he placed third in his prefecture as a senior in sumo wrestling that same year.

He went to Chuo College in Tokyo as a basketball player and studied law. While he had done sumo, he did no amateur wrestling before reading a magazine article in early 1971 about the 1968 Olympics, in particular the Japanese wrestling team. The article inspired him to try amateur wrestling in a quest to participate in the 1976 Olympics. He wasn't of Olympic team calibre in basketball, and sumo wasn't in the Olympics, which led him to amateur wrestling. He actually quit the basketball team to go out for wrestling, a decision that everyone at his college questioned since he was tall and thin. The wrestlers on the team didn't want him and wouldn't let him join in. He was ribbed about his name and his slight physique, and Chuo College already had a star heavyweight Tetsuo Sekigawa, who was the ring leader of those who teased Tsuruta and blocked him from joining the team. (He also later became a famous pro wrestler under the name Mr. Pogo). Tsuruta, pressured away from joining the college team, took up wrestling with an outside club, the Ground Self Defense Force, and picked up the amateur sport, as he later did the pro sport, with miraculous speed. His college team changed its tune and quickly begged him to join. He picked it up so quickly that he won the Japanese collegiate heavyweight championship in both freestyle and Greco-roman in both 1971 and 1972.

He qualified for the Olympic team, and in late August of 1972, went to Munich after only 18 months in the sport. He won his first two matches and then lost via

decision in the third round to place seventh overall.

At 6'4" and about 225 pounds, very large for a Japanese athlete in those days, he came out of the Olympics like a number one draft choice in football. All four wrestling promotions at the time came after him with lucrative offers: the old JWA, (Japanese Wrestling Association) which was in bad financial condition and needed a savior, the IWE (International Wrestling Enterprise), which was affiliated with the AWA in the United State; and the two new groups which had just formed but had most of the major stars, Shohei Baba's All Japan Pro Wrestling (AJPW) and Antonio Inoki's New Japan Pro Wrestling (NJPW).

He was predestined for stardom before ever having a match. Four days after signing with All Japan, he had his first day in wrestling camp under Akio Sato and the late Masio Koma at the new All Japan dojo where he demonstrated an impressive four different types of suplexes. After four months of training, he was sent to Amarillo, TX, to train under then NWA world heavyweight champion Dory Funk Jr., and make his pro debut.

He arrived on March 23, 1973. The Funks knew of his Olympic background, but due to miscommunication and the language barrier, they had no idea he had never actually had a pro wrestling match when they put him in the ring for a television taping the next day against veteran El Gran Tapia.

Tommy Tsuruta, as he was known at the time, became the first Japanese wrestler, and perhaps the only one, to get over as a major draw as a babyface without playing the stereotypical Japanese gimmick in an American territory. His suplexes were so impressive that he became the first wrestler ever in the Amarillo territory to have his moves replayed in slow-motion. His three big suplexes, including what is now known in pro-wrestling as a German suplex, would be taped onto 16mm film, and transferred back in slow-motion mode onto videotape, as they actually didn't have the technology to do it on videotape in those days.

Tsuruta had a unique ability to see almost any maneuver in the ring and duplicate it almost instinctively. He instantly mastered the European uppercut forearm and the spinning toe hold, as well as Jack Brisco's double-arm suplex. He is generally considered the inventor of the missile dropkick and the jumping knee pat. Later, they had him train under Lou Thesz and he used Thesz' trademark Greco-roman backdrop as a regular finisher. Besides the missile dropkick, a move which in the '70s became his domain, he also on occasion did the plancha, a move largely exclusive to very small high flyers in Mexico. He got over so quickly that he was a main eventer only a few weeks after his first match.

Tsuruta got preferential treatment when he returned to Japan. He had signed a big money contract and didn't have to pay the dues a typical Japanese wrestler had to. It would have caused problems within the hierarchy in the traditional Japanese wrestling culture, but Tsuruta was such an impressive athlete that nobody could claim his monster push wasn't deserved. When he debuted in Japan to much fanfare on October 1973 at Korakuen Hall, he was a magnet for resentment from veterans. In his first match, he beat large foreign mid-carder Moose Morowski. His third match in Japan, in 1973 at Tokyo Sumo Hall, saw him and Baba wrestle to a sixty-minute draw when challenging Dory and Terry Funk for the international tag team titles. He was an instant celebrity and the hottest new star in Japanese pro wrestling since Baba and Inoki had gotten over. A contest was held on NTV to give him a nickname, and in late October 1973, Jumbo Tsuruta became a household name. He was kept unbeaten in Japan until the end of January 1974, when he lost challenging for Brisco's NWA title. In 1974, he was voted the best technical wrestler in the world by the Japanese press.

Baba and Tsuruta had replaced Baba and The Destroyer as the top babyface tag team in Japan, and they finally captured the international tag team titles from the Funks in early February 1975 in San Antonio in Tsuruta's first title win. The two teams had numerous main events during that period and for the next eight years. Besides wins over the Funks, the Baba and Tsuruta team became recognized as the top tag team in Japan retaining the belts against teams like Killer Kowalski and Gene Kiniski, Kowalski and Bruno Sammartino, and two wins over Dick the Bruiser and The Crusher. In late 1975, after a loss in a singles match to Baba, Baba announced what everyone had figured, that Tsuruta would some day be his successor. To groom him, the next year would be his

learning year as they would bring the top wrestlers in the world in to face him in singles matches. ▶

Baba and Tsuruta also revived the United National title, the belt that the old JWA had given to Inoki to be a slightly lesser but arguably equal version of the International title that Baba dominated. The idea was that the International title was the king belt, but the great technical wrestlers would wrestle for the UN belt, which Tsuruta dominated from 1976–83. He defended it against the likes of Robinson, Mascaras, Wahoo McDaniel, Ric Flair, Tommy Rich, Ted DiBiase, Dick Slater, Jimmy Snuka and Dick Murdoch. During that period, besides headlining against every major star of the era, he also put out three record albums as a singer and guitar player on the Sony label to capitalize on his mainstream fame.

All Japan in the late '70s and early '80s was built around Baba and Tsuruta as the top stars, feuding with all the top foreigners of the era. But when Ric Flair came to Japan as NWA world champion in October 1981, it was Tsuruta and not Baba that he worked his program with. They had a famous rematch in Japan, a sixty-minute match in June 1983 with Tsuruta taking one fall in a best of three match and thus not winning the title. By 1983, when Tsuruta beat Bruiser Brody to win the International heavyweight title, Tsuruta had quietly taken the top dog spot.

In February 1984 at Sumo Hall in Tokyo, with Terry Funk as referee, he pinned Bockwinkel in thirty-two minutes to win the AWA world heavyweight title in a match with the NWA International title also at stake. He toured

> ▶ **Tsuruta's opponents in 1976 included Greg Gagne,** Rusher Kimura (the top star of the rival IWE in what was a major interpromotional match and was voted Match of the Year – the first of five consecutive years where a Tsuruta match won Match of the Year in Japan), Kintaro Oki (the biggest wrestling star in Korea), Billy Robinson (considered Europe's best wrestler at the time), Jack Brisco, Bobo Brazil, Abdullah the Butcher, Chris Taylor (who also competed in the 1972 Munich Olympics, and finished behind Tsuruta), Terry Funk, Harley Race and Fritz Von Erich.

the United States during a period when AWA business was very strong, headlining shows against the top names in the promotion including Bockwinkel, Blackjack Lanza, Billy Robinson, Jim Brunzell, Greg Gagne and Baron Von Raschke before dropping the title to Rick Martel in May 1984 at the St. Paul Civic Center. Nine days later at the Denen Coliseum in Tokyo, he had a tremendous match against then NWA champion Kerry Von Erich, which went to a double count out.

All Japan was on fire from 1985–1987 when Riki Choshu and his army jumped from New Japan. They introduced a faster-paced style, and Tsuruta, content with the old "big man" heavyweight style, seemed to be passed by Tenryu as the hottest All Japan regular in the top program with Choshu, while Tsuruta worked programs with less interest against the big foreigners. But by 1987, Tsuruta upped his game. Choshu and company had gone back to New Japan, Tenryu was turned heel and their singles feud started. ▶

When Tenryu left the promotion in 1990 to form Super World Sports (SWS) and took a lot of the mid-card wrestlers with him, All Japan had to reinvent itself, and Tsuruta ushered in the modern era in June 1990 when he was pinned by Misawa before 14,800 fans at Budokan Hall. The win made Misawa the hottest wrestler in the country and All Japan caught fire for the next few years with Tsuruta and Misawa on top, both in key singles matches which Tsuruta usually won. The Misawa win over Tsuruta, which came a few hundred tickets shy of capacity, was the last All Japan show not to sell out in Tokyo for the next several years. Tsuruta chose Akira Taue as his tag team partner for classics with Misawa and Kawada, before the illness that ended his career. His last important main event was in October of 1992, at the All Japan company's 20th anniversary show at Budokan Hall, where he teamed with Terry Gordy and André the Giant to beat Baba and Hansen and Dory. He finally had pinned his teacher. His final pro match was on September 11, 1998 at Budokan Hall in a mid-card comedy match teaming with Baba and Kimura against Tsuyoshi Kikuchi and Masa Fuchi and Haruka Eigen.

▶ **Tsuruta vs. Tenryu on top started a trend that has lasted until the present where All Japan** presented the best singles main events held anywhere in the world. Tsuruta was the catalyst for Baba cutting down to two major titles, a singles Triple Crown and the Double tag team (combining the PWF World tag team titles with the long-existing NWA International belts). The tag belts were unified in 1988 when Tsuruta and Yoshiaki Yatsu (who represented Japan in the 1980 Olympics), known as "The Olympics," beat Tenryu and Ashura Hara on June 4 in Sapporo for the PWF (Pacific Wrestling Federation) belts, and then on June 10 at Budokan Hall beat The Road Warriors for the International belts, and began a feud with Hansen and Terry Gordy. The Triple Crown unification came in April 1989 at the Tokyo Ota Ward Gymnasium. Tsuruta won the International title from Bruiser Brody in April 1988, then defeated Hansen, who held both the United National and PWF belts in the unification match, and then feuded with Tenryu, Hansen, Gordy, Williams and Misawa over it until his career as a headliner was over. He had his only major singles match with Kobashi in January 1990, and his famous singles match with Kawada was in January 1992.

Gordon Solie

Gordon Solie passed away from brain cancer on June 28, 2000 at the age of 71. His distinctive voice had been the trademark of pro wrestling in the Southeast for more than two decades and in some ways the symbol of pro wrestling in the '70s. He announced more pro wrestling matches on television than any man who ever lived.

His ability to give pro wrestling credibility as legitimate athletic competition was the forerunner of today's Jim Ross, and his underplayed style of selling wrestling was a complete contrast to the modern game.

Solie's health had been failing for four years prior to his death, since his retirement in 1996 as the host of Ring Warriors, a syndicated version of New Japan Pro Wrestling which aired on Eurosport. Solie was a believer in pro wrestling maintaining athletic credibility and in later years he would show subtle disdain when the product had gotten, in his view, out of hand.

In October of 2000, Solie was diagnosed with cancer of the larynx. He gave up smoking after 55 years. He was down to 135 pounds, and was just content to let it take its course. Intensely private about his personal life, he knew the end was near and didn't want to become a sympathetic character to the public, so he asked that wrestling friends Don Curtis, Brian Blair, Howard Brody and Lou Thesz keep it quiet. Indeed, few outside his inner circle knew.

Solie, who during his career announced an estimated 25,000 televised wrestling matches, was best known as the host of Georgia Championship Wrestling and its Sunday "Best of" counterpart (renamed World Championship Wrestling in 1982 due to its expanding audience and the promotion's attempted expansion) from 1973 through 1985. ▶

At various periods in the '70s and '80s, the Florida shows Solie announced were syndicated outside of Florida into major markets, including New York and even St. Louis. In addition, Solie would often do the taped match and interview, building up the arrival of the world champion into a territory. So even before cable, Solie was the pre-eminent voice of NWA wrestling and was synonymous to fans with wrestling in the states of Florida and Georgia.

"His whole life was dedicated to wrestling," said long-time friend Don Curtis, who wrestled in Florida and for years promoted weekly shows in Jacksonville. He noted Solie really didn't have a lot of hobbies outside of wrestling. "He came up with ideas and programs. He dedicated his life to wrestling. He believed in the product and in what he said. Because people recognized that, they believed him. When he said something, the people believed it was true because they respected him so much. That's all he really wanted to do was to make it (wrestling) better."

> ▶ **WTCG (now TBS), Ted Turner's Channel 17 in** Atlanta, had gotten the local wrestling franchise in 1972 and within one year was airing two different companies in a famous promotional war.
>
> The station later launched the first attempt at a true national cable SuperStation. As more and more systems picked up the station in the late '70s, the trademark three weekly hours of GCW, a two hour show taped earlier that day that aired at 6:05 PM Eastern time on Saturday, and a one hour highlight show that aired at 6:05 PM on Sunday, became the first cable television shows to consistently be viewed in more than one million homes. The show peaked nationally in 1981, when it averaged a 6.4 rating for the year. It drew numbers no wrestling show on cable ever approached again until the WWF.

FORMER NWA WORLD CHAMPIONS LOU THESZ, COWBOY DICK HUTTON,
GENE KINISKI AND GORDON SOLIE (LEFT TO RIGHT)

Born on January 26, 1929 in Minneapolis and adopted shortly thereafter by the Solie family, he migrated to Florida in 1950 after serving time in the Air Force working with Armed Forces Radio. He was working as a disc jockey, reporter and talk show host for a small Tampa radio station as well as the stadium voice of sprint car and stock car races in the area. In the early '50s, he got hired on as the ring announcer for Cowboy Luttrell's weekly matches in Tampa for $5 per night, and later expanded his duties to helping with advertising and

▶ "Other announcers at the time treated wrestling like a comedy act," Solie said in an interview a few days before his death. "When I got the job, I went to Cowboy Luttrell and asked him how he wanted me to handle it. He looked me in the eye and said, 'It's like your paycheck. Treat it very seriously.' That's what I did."

publicity. He didn't grow up as a wrestling fan, but learned the game during that period and got his break in 1960 when he was hired to announce the weekly television show in Tampa, which the next year was syndicated on videotape throughout the state. ▶

Solie then spent a few weeks training with the wrestlers, in particular Eddie Graham and John Heath, having them stretch him and put him into holds so he would know what every one was supposed to feel like. With his knowledge of anatomy, he could sell the pain and psychology of the moves, which he correctly called, sometimes to a fault, to the viewing audience to portray wrestling as a legitimate sporting event. Solie until the end was the last man in wrestling to use the term "suplay," still used in the amateurs, which is the correct pronunciation of the original French word spelled suplex.

Solie was often compared to Vin Scully, considered the pre-eminent baseball announcer of the same period. He was anything but bombastic. In a world of weird, he dressed well, was known for his verbiage, and had a style that made the media types steer clear of disrespect. He treated wrestling as a sport, doing anything to tie athletic credibility to the product, which was the basis of the successful Florida operation. He also always tried to find a thread of reality in the sometimes goofy angles. As announcer, he was one of the most successful salesmen wrestling had. Wrestlers came and went from Florida for decades but he was the constant, and considered himself something of the star maker. Once, when Lex Luger, whom the Florida company was built around for a year, was signed to a big money contract by Crockett, Solie bragged that he was the one who made Luger, and he'd just as easily make Ron Simmons (who was being given Luger's spot).

He made the world title seem like, well...the world title, and he made the quest for it seem like the chase for the holy grail. There is little question that perhaps the most famous NWA title program of that era was the Jack Brisco three-plus-year chase of Dory Funk Jr. in the early '70s. The lengthy matches, including frequent sixty-minute ones, popularized one of his famous trademark lines about classic pro wrestling matches, calling them "human chess at its finest."

His reputation as the best announcer in wrestling picked up steam outside of Florida with his call of the July 11, 1964 match where Hiro Matsuda won the NWA junior heavyweight title from Danny Hodge in Tampa. In those days, because world title changes were so rare (Hodge had held the title for four years), the tape was sent to many of the NWA offices around the country and aired on numerous television shows. Leroy McGuirk, who promoted out of Tulsa and was the booker of the

junior heavyweight champion, and was blind, told Solie as he listened to him that it was the first time in years he could see a match. Solie said that was the greatest single moment of his wrestling career.

The second biggest moment was on May 21, 1995 in St. Petersburg, when WCW inducted Solie into its Hall of Fame at the Slamboree PPV show. It was a very trying period because it was at the very end of his tenure with the company and he was having a hard time coming to grips with a business that was rapidly changing. ▶

He finally agreed to do it, because it was his job, but it would be the final straw that would lead to his departure from WCW for good.

That night, after inductions of Wahoo McDaniel, Terry Funk, Antonio Inoki, Dusty Rhodes, Angelo Poffo and John Studd, he was told to stay out there for one last induction. Wrestling legend has it that Solie was unaware of who it would be. He acted shocked, putting on a great emotional performance for the fans who grew up to his voice for generations, and actually stole the entire show. That aspect of it was a work. Solie did know about it ahead of time. It was his second proudest moment as he stood there in front of people in his home market giving him a standing ovation, and Lou Thesz told him, "Enjoy it. You deserve it."

The week after Slamboree, Solie spoke his mind about the Hall of Fame, and that was the end of his announcing career in the United States. After the blow-up with Eric Bischoff, he had two shows left to voice-over. He

---

▶ **Due to his image as "the dean of wrestling announcers," as he was nicknamed, Solie had** been used to inducting various wrestlers into a WCW Hall of Fame. The selections, which started a few years earlier with the likes of Lou Thesz and Verne Gagne, had become very political, and before the show Solie was upset about having to announce the introductions of two of the candidates, John Studd and Angelo Poffo. Poffo, who was a wrestling star in the Midwest but hardly had a Hall of Fame career, was inducted simply as a favor to his son, Randy Savage. There was also a problem with Studd, who had passed away just two months earlier and had lots of friends in the organization and was well-liked within wrestling. Studd's big national run was in the WWF and Solie felt it was supposed to be a Hall of Fame for the history of the NWA and WCW wrestling. The business itself was coming off the steroid trial of Vince McMahon and still somewhat engulfed in that controversy. Studd's doctor had just gone on ABC's Wide World of Sports in a much-publicized segment a week or two before, and tied Studd's steroid usage to the cancer that claimed his life at an early age. He felt that it was wrong to induct Studd into the Hall of Fame, because it was so soon after the news of the nature of Studd's death.

GOOD FRIENDS GORDON SOLIE AND KILLER KOWALSKI IN LOS ANGELES

fans. It came as a total shock when one day, Freddy Miller was introducing McMahon and Gorilla Monsoon in the famed TBS studios in downtown Atlanta, and tapes were airing of WWF matches filmed in Canada. After the first WWF show aired on July 14, 1984, actually nicknamed "Black Saturday" there was a furor from fans nationwide, but particularly in the Southeast. The complaints by and large were not about any of the wrestlers who abruptly disappeared from sight. The complaints, and there were thousands, were that they wanted their Georgia wrestling back, and in particular they wanted Gordon Solie. McMahon, sensing a major public relations problem since Solie's name was in so many of the complaints, responded by saying publicly he was negotiating to bring Solie in. Solie was working for so many different regional NWA stations at the time that it would have been very difficult to get him to make the move.

But the phone calls and complaints to TBS were so strong that two weeks later Ted Turner made a decision, which was probably the beginning of the end of the Turner/McMahon relationship. He added a third show in the prime time of 7:35 PM, called Championship Wrestling from Georgia, a new company headed by Anderson, which put Solie back on the station and created yet an additional hour of wrestling on the SuperStation that would last more than ten years.

On January 20, 1973, Solie showed up as the new voice of Championship Wrestling from Georgia. He simply said he was sitting in that week for Sterling Brewer. One month later, his name was in the opening of the show. He remained on the station in that time slot until McMahon took over in 1984. Soon after that, Solie was commuting every Tuesday to Columbus, GA to tape another syndicated show that aired in Savannah, Augusta and Columbus so the NWA group in the smaller markets would have two separate television shows. Ray Gunkel,

told friends that had he still worked with the company, he would have quit for sure a few months later when the company did what he considered the worst angle ever, where The Giant fell off the roof of Cobo Arena at that year's Halloween Havoc PPV, only to show up later in the show, wrestling Hulk Hogan in the main event.

The biggest testament to his personal popularity with the fans was in the summer of 1984, when Vince McMahon bought majority interest in Georgia Championship Wrestling Inc. (GCW) in a hostile takeover, then folded the company itself. He kept its most important contract, giving it national exposure for three hours on TBS, inheriting the time slot of the most watched wrestling show in the country. Jack and Gerald Brisco were the first GCW stockholders to sell, frustrated because they could see national promotions were going to be the order of the day. McMahon had already started his expansion and felt no qualms about stepping on toes.

The number of people aware of McMahon buying majority interest and the court battles by Ole Anderson attempting to stop the take-over, which would have been gigantic news today, were unknown to virtually all wrestling

AT A TAMPA, FLORIDA REUNION – MR. AND MRS. DON CURTIS,
GORDON SOLIE, JOHN TOLOS AND FORMER WOMEN'S WRESTLING
CHAMPION ELLA WALDECK

who managed to negotiate a slot on WTCG (which became WTBS) at 7 PM on Saturdays, following the NWA show, went out of business in late 1974.

Within two years, more and more cable companies started adding Atlanta's Channel 17. By 1980, Channel 17 had topped 15 million homes nationwide and one million of them were watching the wrestling show, the hottest program in the infancy of what is now known as cable television.

When promoters were able to bring in some of the wrestlers off the Atlanta television program, they showed a noticeable increase at the gate. Wrestling had changed forever. Ole Anderson, who controlled the TV, felt the exposure could lead to going national. Vince McMahon Sr., apparently aware of what was happening, then raided Anderson of some of his top talent including Paul Orndorff and the Masked Superstar, and the Georgia business locally started faltering, causing dissension among the stockholders. In late 1983, McMahon started the destruction of the system for good.

As the years went by, maintaining that dignified aura while doing the broadcasts, as the angles got less and less credible, became at first difficult and then impossible. It became clear that by the mid-'80s, as the business was changing, that Solie's performance lacked the focus and inspiration that made him the legend among announcers and garnered his well-known nickname as "The Walter Cronkite of Wrestling." At first, he was no longer winning Announcer of the Year awards that had previously been a given. Then he was no longer even considered among the best. Solie began losing jobs in wrestling. This was blamed more on his work suffering from drinking than on his refusal to overhype.

Around then, a series of political maneuvers took place. Turner approached Bill Watts with a deal and added yet another promotion to his SuperStation line-up. (Embarrassingly for McMahon, the new Watts show, which only lasted 13 weeks, was drawing better ratings than the WWF broadcasts in the same time slot.) At this point, the idea was for Watts to take over McMahon's traditional wrestling time slot on the station. However, Jim Barnett brokered a deal which brought McMahon and Crockett together, with Crockett buying out the rights to

McMahon's time slots and also getting exclusivity on the station. Watts got screwed out of national exposure in the process. He quickly sold his company to Crockett about 18 months before Crockett himself went broke. Solie was no longer even part of the SuperStation equation at this point, working for *Continental, Pro Wrestling this Week* and *Florida*. When he got the word about Crockett, who had just taken over Florida, his first words were, "Let's see how long I'll have a job with them."

When Crockett bought the SuperStation time slot two years earlier, just before the change took place from WWF programming to what was then Mid Atlantic programming, the Saturday Georgia early morning show saw Solie simply announce, "I'll be away on business next week." After 13 years of being the state's, and in many ways the nation's weekend wrestling constant, that was how transitions were handled in those days. Tony Schiavone was host the next week with Solie's name never mentioned again. Solie's weekly announcing in Florida also ended at the hands of Crockett, who bought the dying Florida territory and, with the bitterness of the SuperStation dismissal, had another falling out. Crockett cut back the weekly TV tapings to do bi-weekly tapings of two hours each in a cost-cutting move. Because there were fewer tapings, he felt he could lower Solie's salary because he was working half the dates. Solie felt because it was the same number of shows, that shouldn't be the case, and just like that, after 27 years, he was gone. Solie complained bitterly about the dismissal, noting that after all that time, he didn't even get a Timex watch as a going away present.

After that, Solie's announcing duties were limited to Continental Championship Wrestling based in Alabama, a job he first started in September of 1975 and kept until 1988.

The Florida show was, in its glory days, taped on Thursdays. The Atlanta show was traditionally taped from 10 AM to noon on Saturday mornings, since Atlanta ran its house shows on Friday nights and thus the national talent flown in for the big shows would already be in town. Solie would have to do interviews and wrap-arounds as well as some slots for the Sunday "Best of" show, so he'd usually get out of the Atlanta studios at 1 PM. Making plane connections to Dothan, AL, where he did a live show on Saturday afternoons at 5:30 PM Central Time, wasn't easy.

He resurfaced as a part-owner, and of course as the voice, of a new Florida promotion with Mike Graham, Steve Keirn, and later Dusty Rhodes. Rhodes and Solie were intertwined in the minds of every wrestling fan in Florida during the '70s when they were the stars of the show, as well as in Georgia where Rhodes was the top draw. While the two would joke about being the Howard Cosell/Muhammad Ali of pro wrestling, they were not friends off television. Solie was never part-owner of the CWF (Championship Wrestling from Florida) promotion, although legend always had him in that position. Solie later recognized that the story was created and spread by Eddie Graham so no promoter would attempt to steal Solie from Florida.

After Crockett sold to Turner, there was a movement by many people who had been friends of his to bring Solie back to WCW in 1989, simply to do a weekly wrestling news feature. He stayed with the company until the 1995 break-up under Eric Bischoff.

DAVE MELTZER is considered the pioneer of pro wrestling journalism. A lifelong fan, Meltzer began writing about the sport at the age of ten in various newsletters and fan club publications. His *California Wrestling Report* and *International Wrestling Gazette* in the 70s were considered two of the top underground wrestling publications. While attending San Jose State University and reporting for the *Oakland Tribune*, Meltzer started the *Wrestling Observer Newsletter* in 1982. It was the first publication regularly covering pro wrestling that made no bones about the industry being "athletic entertainment," a term he coined (later changed to "sports entertainment" by Vince McMahon).

While the publication was read by virtually every major decision-maker in pro wrestling from very early on, he was criticized for breaking kayfabe – an ancient code never to admit that even the most blatantly silly scenarios were planned in advance and that winners and losers of matches were predetermined. The wildly popular newsletter spawned the base of what later became known as "smart fans." Now the vast majority of the audience, these fans attend pro wrestling events fully knowledgeable that what they are seeing is scripted entertainment, and enjoy it for what it is instead of what it pretends to be. Through his newsletter, Meltzer was responsible for educating a generation of fans and many future wrestlers as to what the industry was really about, as well as exposing Americans to pro wrestling in Japan and Mexico.

The *Observer* quickly became the publication of record in the pro wrestling industry, a position it maintains to this day. After nearly 20 years, Meltzer still puts out the newsletter, with its trademark small type and lengthy reporting, on a weekly basis. It has been ranked in the newsletter field many times as one of the top newsletters of any kind in the United States, and Meltzer himself has been ranked highly in many polls as one of the most influential people in the wrestling industry worldwide.

Meltzer grew up in California and graduated with a journalism degree from San Jose State University. He worked for several newspapers from 1981 to 1987 before leaving the field to make the *Observer* a full-time endeavor. He has been quoted as the leading pro wrestling expert in the nation in virtually every major form of media, including the *New York Times, Los Angeles Times, TV Guide, Newsweek* and *Sports Illustrated*. His television appearances include stints on the CBS Evening News, ABC World News Tonight, numerous appearances on Entertainment Tonight, and on documentaries on pro wrestling on The Discovery Channel, A&E and Court TV. He was also featured in the two most widely acclaimed documentaries on the inside of the pro wrestling business, "Hitman Hart: Wrestling with Shadows," and "Beyond the Mat." He is currently part of the crew at Live Audio Wrestling, a Toronto-based, twice-weekly talk show that covers the wrestling industry. In 1996, he started the Wrestling Observer Hall of Fame, the most respected pro wrestling hall of fame in the world, with the top wrestlers, promoters, historians and writers voting on inclusion with similar standards to the Baseball Hall of Fame.

The Wrestling Observer Newsletter, the No. 1 insider pro wrestling publication in the world, is available either by ordering through the mail or through credit card orders. The mailing address is Wrestling Observer, P.O. Box 1228, Campbell, CA 95009-1228. You can send credit card orders to dave@wrestlingobserver.com You can order by mail via check or money order made out to Wrestling Observer, or via cash. For credit card orders, send your name, address, phone number, credit card information and an expiration date. There will be a $1 processing fee for all credit card orders. Rates for the Observer are:

UNITED STATES

$11 for 4 weekly issues, $28 for 12, $54 for 24, $90 for 40

CANADA AND MEXICO

$12 for 4 weekly issues, $30 for 12, $57 for 24, $95 for 40

REST OF THE WORLD

$14 for 4 weekly issues, $36 for 12, $72 for 24, $120 for 40

For those who live in Europe, you can get the fastest delivery and best rates by sending to grapplingactio@aol.com.

For more information about The Wrestling Observer Newsletter and daily wrestling news, interviews and features visit www.wrestlingobserver.com.